Ricardian Politics

✣

Murray Milgate
AND
Shannon C. Stimson

PRINCETON UNIVERSITY PRESS

PRINCETON, NEW JERSEY

Copyright ©1991 by Princeton University Press
Published by Princeton University Press, 41 William Street,
Princeton, New Jersey 08540
In the United Kingdom: Princeton University Press, Oxford
All Rights Reserved

Library of Congress Cataloging-in-Publication Data

Milgate, Murray.
Ricardian politics / Murray Milgate and Shannon C. Stimson.
p.   cm.
Includes bibliographical references (p.   ) and index.
ISBN 0-691-04278-0 (alk. paper)
1. Ricardo, David, 1772–1823—Contributions in political science.
I. Stimson, Shannon C. II. Title.
JC223.R53M55   1991
320'.092—dc20   91-19461   CIP

This book has been composed in Linotron Caledonia

Princeton University Press books are printed on acid-free paper,
and meet the guidelines for permanence and durability of the
Committee on Production Guidelines for Book Longevity of the
Council on Library Resources

Printed in the United States of America by Princeton University Press,
Princeton, New Jersey

1   3   5   7   9   10   8   6   4   2

From "The Masque of Anarchy," by Percy Bysshe Shelley. Written on the occasion of the massacre at Manchester (Peterloo), 1819.

"Let a great Assembly be
Of the fearless and the free
On some spot of English ground
Where the plains stretch wide around.

"Let the blue sky overhead,
The green earth on which ye tread,
All that must eternal be
Witness the solemnity.

"From the corners uttermost
Of the bounds of English coast;
From every hut, village and town
Where those who live and suffer moan
For others' misery or their own,

"From the workhouse and the prison,
Where pale as corpses newly risen,
Women, children, young and old
Groan for pain, and weep for cold—

"From the haunts of daily life
Where is waged the daily strife
With common wants and common cares
Which sows the human heart with tares—

"Lastly from the palaces
Where the murmur of distress
Echoes, like the distant sound
Of a wind alive around

"Those prison halls of wealth and fashion
Where some few feel such compassion
For those who groan, and toil, and wail
As must make their brethren pale—

"Ye who suffer woes untold,
Or to feel, or to behold
Your lost country bought and sold
With a price of blood and gold—

"Let a vast assembly be,
And with great solemnity
Declare with measured words that ye
Are, as God has made ye, free—"

✣ *Contents* ✣

✤ Preface ✤

Few deny that the work of economists has often embodied or stimulated significant contributions to political thought. The writings of Smith, Marx, Schumpeter, Keynes, Hayek, and Friedman are but a few of the more prominent examples. However, the work of the great classical economist David Ricardo is not usually placed in such company. Despite Ricardo's affiliations with philosophical radicals like Bentham and James Mill, the most that previous scholars have been prepared to allow is that if Ricardo spoke to political questions at all, he sought only to address issues of economic policy. That Ricardo might have articulated a distinctive political vision has not been seriously considered. Nor has the idea that this vision might have been grounded on a novel and sophisticated linkage of arguments for democratic reform with conclusions of political economy been explored. Quite simply, there has been almost no examination of Ricardo's politics (which were lucid and considerable) nor any sustained examination of the character of a 'Ricardian' politics in which the case for more representative and democratic government might be systematically structured by economic thought. It is as a contribution towards the filling of this gap in the existing literature that the present work is offered.

In certain respects, the picture of Ricardo that emerges in these pages may be unfamiliar to some readers. We present a Ricardo who spoke explicitly not only to the immediate political questions of his day, but one who also addressed some of the larger political themes of early nineteenth-century democratic thought. Thus, Ricardo both confronted and engaged the issues dominating British parliamentary debate in the first decades of the century. The limits of popular protest, religious toleration, colonial administration, postwar reconstruction, and the Irish question, as well as the more explicit questions of economic policy, including banking regulation, governmental expenditure, and the burden of taxation, all came under Ricardo's scrutiny. In examining these issues, Ricardo systematically reconsidered and reformulated both the Whig and Radical theories of representation, political citizenship, and the foundations of political stability. Examined in this light, Ricardo's contribution to political thought has a legitimate claim to being ranked alongside those of the better-known political economists of the past. It is just as important to state that this is not an account of Ricardo drawn from our having simply re-interpreted existing scholarship. Rather, we have brought to bear on the question evidence of Ricardo's more systematic political reflections which are to be found in writings that have been (for the most part) previously neglected.

It should be said, however, that we see ourselves as being engaged not only in the recovery of a more accurate version of Ricardo's political thinking, but also as contributing to the enterprise of securing a clearer understanding of the relationship between economic and political philosophy (and actual historical change) in an epoch that saw, at once, the consolidation of modern capitalist society, and the emergence of modern democratic political ideology in Britain. More recent scholarship in this area has tended to move away from a focus on the economic element in the development of political thought and, accordingly, has placed greater emphasis on factors such as religion, culture, locality, and the discourse of republican virtue. While we have no wish to depreciate the value of this impressive body of work, it does seem to us that this tendency may have gone a little too far. The consequence appears to have been to place more 'traditional' factors in the forefront of the account of the democratic movement. The story of democratization that unfolds is often presented as one of a clash between traditional aspirations and values and the economic necessities of an emergent industrial society. Doubtless there is much truth in this. However, in the case of Ricardo, one finds another element at work as well. For in Ricardo's more explicitly political writing, one encounters an attempt to construct an argument for democratic reform that is at once based upon, and consistent with, an account of the operation of the new market mechanism itself. Considered from this perspective, Ricardo emerges in this writing as a more truly nineteenth-century thinker than many of his contemporaries. Ricardo was someone whose debt to the eighteenth century should be measured more by the extent of his departure from the traditional discourse of eighteenth-century politics than by an adherence to it. In this way, one finds in Ricardo a new and unrepentantly 'modern' argument for the basis of democratic reform.

There is one more thing that should be said. It is that we came to this enterprise almost entirely without any preconceptions as to what we would find. Almost, that is, because like everyone else who has heard of Ricardo, we had been brought up on a diet consisting of the various caricatures of him which fill the secondary literature on the economic and political thought of the period; and it had made us feel somewhat uneasy. But despite our disquiet over these caricatures, our intention throughout has been to *recover* Ricardo's politics, and to present what we actually found in Ricardo's writing, not what we thought he might have had in mind. This does not mean that we have avoided interpretation. Quite the opposite. While our primary task was conceived as being one of outlining and clarifying the main features of Ricardo's thinking about politics, of elaborating the relationship in which this stood with respect to his economics, and of situating all of this within the context of early philosophic-radical thought, our ultimate goal was to come away from that exercise with a reasonably satisfying vision of something one could justifiably call Ricardian politics.

We should, however, alert the reader to the fact that our use of the idea of a Ricardian politics is not to be confused with existing (and, as we see it, ill-adapted) uses of the term 'Ricardian'. Indeed, this term has been used to categorize the thinking of writers as diverse as J. R. McCulloch, James Mill, Thomas Hodgskin, and Thomas De Quincey. Instead, our presentation of Ricardian politics involves us in delineating a quite precise framework of concepts. As we have already said, a major part of our intention has been to highlight the distinctiveness of Ricardo's own politics and to establish the larger, conceptual framework which surrounds it. If we have provided an accurate picture of his politics, then we would claim that we have also established a distinctive vision of Ricardian politics into which McCulloch, Mill, and other putative 'Ricardians' do not fit neatly. Indeed, we have worked throughout to eradicate the kind of associational method which has served in the past only to obscure or distort Ricardo's own position. Whether we have been entirely successful in this endeavour or not, is something for others to judge. For our part, we should probably guage our efforts to have been worthwhile if they acted as nothing more than a stimulus to both political theorists and historians of economic thought to re-think the suitability of the niche into which they have consigned Ricardo's contribution to the political and economic underpinnings of early nineteenth-century democratic reform.

Finally, we have refrained as far as possible in the body of the text from attempting to have Ricardo's voice speak directly to contemporary political discourse. With one or two exceptions (which are clearly signaled), the only place we have allowed ourselves the luxury of a measure of that sort of speculation, is in the final chapter. But by then, we trust, we have laid Ricardo's cards on the table. Although we have then played out the hand as we think fit, the reader is under no obligation to follow us.

In writing this book we have accumulated a number of debts which it is only proper for us to acknowledge. The extensive collections of early nineteenth-century economic and political literature in the main libraries at Harvard—Widener Library, Hilles Library, and the Kress Collection—made our research less arduous than it would have been. To these we would add the collections of the University Library at Cambridge (where Ricardo's papers are housed), the Marshall Library at Cambridge, and the Goldsmiths' Library at the University of London. We are also indebted to Donald Winch and A. W. Coats for comments on an earlier version of this manuscript. It goes almost without saying that, like all students of Ricardo, we owe most to the superb scholarly edition of his *Works and Correspondence* left to us by the Royal Economic Society and its editor, Piero Sraffa.

M.M. & S.C.S.
April 1991

✤ Note on References ✤

THE BIBLIOGRAPHY provides the full publication details of all the works (and editions of works) to which reference is made throughout this volume. When a book, article, or essay is cited in a footnote we have adopted the convention of giving the author's name only on those occasions when the authorship is not apparent from the passage in the text to which the note is appended. Each time a work is cited, we have utilized an abbreviated form of its title (though one which is easily traceable in the bibliography). In the case of writings by Ricardo, all of which are taken from the eleven volumes of Piero Sraffa's edition of *The Works and Correspondence of David Ricardo* published by Cambridge University Press for the Royal Economic Society, we have again used abbreviated forms for titles (where they exist) and our citation practice is to give the relevant volume and page number. Extracts from the correspondence are cited in the customary form: giving the names of the correspondents, the direction of the exchange, the full date of the letter, and the volume and page in which it can be found in the Sraffa edition. References to Ricardo's parliamentary speeches are cited in footnotes by giving the title of the volume of the *Works* in which they are assembled (that is, the fifth volume, entitled *Speeches and Evidence*), the date on which they were delivered, and the page on which they can be found in that volume. Other citations from parliamentary proceedings almost invariably follow *Hansard*. Citations from the Supplement to the 4th, 5th, and 6th editions of the *Encyclopedia Britannica* follow the title of the article actually printed in the Supplement.

Ricardian Politics

✤

The Case of Ricardo

IN THE HISTORY of philosophical radicalism, David Ricardo stands as an enigmatic figure. Look around, and you will find many caricatures of Ricardo. If, for instance, we are to take what seems to be the majority opinion at its word, Ricardo was politically naïve. As the economist's economist, he is said to have been concerned exclusively with 'directing government to right measures',[1] somewhat in the manner of an appeal to the right reason of existing political powers—whoever those powers might be and however they might be constituted. A leading species of this particular rendering is the idea that Ricardo just did not trouble himself overly with politics.[2] In other accounts, Ricardo's political thinking is seen to be derivative and unoriginal. The dominant notion here seems to be that Ricardo was little more than James Mill's marionette (or, perhaps, his amanuensis) when it came to the expression of political sentiment.[3] Still another view, favoured in certain

---

[1] *Letter to Trower*, 12 November 1819, in *Works and Correspondence*, 8:132. See also the *Letter to Brown*, 13 October 1919, 8:100, where Ricardo remarks that the 'science' of political economy can be deployed to expose 'our errors of legislation on subject of trade'. This seems to be the theme of what is the best and most comprehensive examination of Ricardo in parliament available, Barry Gordon's *Political Economy in Parliament*. Similarly, Donald Winch appears to see Ricardo as treating economics as 'the science of the legislator' very much in the orthodox fashion, although it must be said that he appears to be the only one to have discussed at any length at all Ricardo's purely political writings (*That Noble Science of Politics*, pp. 106–7).

[2] Consider Schumpeter, who asserted that although Ricardo is usually described as a utilitarian, 'he was not one'; and this, 'not because of his having had another philosophy', but rather 'because that busy and positive mind had no philosophy at all' (*History of Economic Analysis*, p. 471). In a somewhat similar vein, Mark Blaug writes in his *Ricardian Economics* that 'Ricardo had never paid much attention to the scope and functions of government' (p. 193).

[3] This opinion was widely canvassed by John Stuart Mill who remarked that his father had 'induced' Ricardo to enter parliament where 'he rendered so much service to his and my father's opinions on political economy and on other subjects' (*Autobiography*, p. 19). The theme was re-iterated by Leslie Stephen who characterized Ricardo in parliament as a 'defender' of established utilitarian doctrines

Marxist circles, is that Ricardianism is synonymous with apologetics. Here Ricardo is portrayed as the friend of the bourgeoisie, the champion of interests of the rising capitalist class against the interests of both the old aristocracy and the new (and growing) proletariat.[4] It seems hardly necessary to add that there are many accounts which offer some combination of these views. One thing, however, is clear. Such attitudes share a common ingredient: not one of them could be said to take seriously Ricardo's contributions to the field of politics and, more specifically, to political thought.

It will be immediately apparent the extent to which these caricatures are conformable to the familiar portrait of Ricardo as the ultra-abstract economic theorist who, as his contemporary Henry Brougham first claimed, gave the impression of having dropped from another planet.[5] Given the ubiquity of this im-

(*The English Utilitarians*, 2:27). Arnold Toynbee asserted that 'Ricardo's political opinions in fact merely reflect those of James Mill' (*Lectures*, p. 127). Elie Halévy followed suit, arguing that '[a]ll the actions in Ricardo's life, after 1811, were willed by James Mill' and that, in particular, Ricardo had made Mill's argument from the essay on *Government* 'his own' in a speech in parliament in 1823 (*Philosophic Radicalism*, pp. 266, 421). The legend begins with Bentham's claim to the 'spiritual' parentage of Mill, and Mill's 'spiritual' parentage of Ricardo. Upon Ricardo's death, James Mill wrote to McCulloch that Ricardo had had 'hardly a thought or a purpose, respecting either public, or his private affairs, in which I was not his confidant and adviser' (*Letter to McCulloch*, 19 September 1823, 9:390).

[4] The substance of the charge is familiar enough, though Marx himself never accused Ricardo of being an apologist (an epithet he reserved for figures such as Nassau Senior). Ricardo stands charged with identifying the interests of one particular class of society with the interests of the whole of society; he is 'the most classic representative . . . of the bourgeoisie and the most stoical adversary of the proletariat' (Marx to Weydemeyer, 5 March 1852, *Selected Correspondence*, p. 57). It is perhaps worth noticing that this charge did not have to await the advent of Marx's criticism of bourgeois political economy to be levelled against Ricardo. It was regularly brought against him in parliament by his opponents; in particular, he was often charged with having only the interests of the 'mercantile' class at heart. For some of Ricardo's parliamentary replies to such criticism see *Works and Correspondence*, 5:81–82, 87, 317–18, 471. See also his *Letter to Trower*, 28 December 1819 (8:147–48).

[5] Brougham made the remark in a speech to the House of Commons (30 May 1820) supporting a motion for the establishment of a select committee to examine the question of agricultural distress. It is quoted in Ricardo's *Works and Correspondence* 5:56. Brougham was rather more gentle in his later sketch of Ricardo in parliament: 'his views were often, indeed, abundantly theoretical, sometimes too refined for his audience, occasionally extravagant from his propensity to fol-

age,[6] it is scarcely surprising that David Ricardo's politics have not been admitted as a serious topic of conversation among either historians of economic or political thought. Unfortunately, however, if this-worldliness had anything at all to do with deciding the matter, one would be faced with quite a number of paradoxes. After all, Ricardo was at once a successful London stockbroker and practising politician of some consequence. On the criterion of worldliness Ricardo would probably rank higher than most of the great economists either before him or since. Think of Adam Smith; there was someone whose entire life was passed in the other-worldly environments of the university, the entourage of an aristocrat, and the isolated little fishing village of Kirkcaldy—who never wrote a single 'topical pamphlet' and but a few very early 'learned reviews'.[7] If any of the classical economists might be said to have fallen from another planet, it would surely be Adam Smith. Nevertheless, whether with intentions benign or mischievous, paradox has not been allowed to stand in the way of Ricardo image-building,[8] and in one guise or another Brougham's sketch of Ricardo has come down to us today almost unaltered.

---

low a right principle into all its consequences, without duly taking into account in practice the condition of things to which he was applying it, as if a mechanician were to construct an engine without taking into account the resistance of the air in which it was to work' (*Works and Correspondence* 5:xxxiii). Over the next one hundred and fifty years, this same theme surfaces again and again. For example, in *Ricardo on Taxation*, Carl Shoup warned of Ricardo's 'passion for intellectual exercise' (p. 252) even when dealing with a subject so obviously practical as taxation.

[6] Exception must be made here for Edwin Cannan who argued in his *History of Theories of Production and Distribution* that '[a]mong all the delusions which prevail as to the history of English political economy there is none greater than the belief that the economics of the Ricardian school and period were of an almost wholly abstract and unpractical character' (p. 383). At the far extreme of this line of thinking is Max Beer, who actually claimed that '[a]mong the theorists of Political Economy there has been none more inductive, and less abstract in method, than Ricardo (*History of British Socialism* 1:147); a view which, it must be said, seems to be just as fanciful as its long-established alternative.

[7] Donald Winch, 'The Enlightenment and the science of the legislator', p. 28.

[8] Walter Bagehot, who promulgated essentially the same image of Ricardo fifty years after Brougham had invented it, quickly spotted these paradoxes. However, not to be deterred from his purpose by taking them seriously, he determined to deploy them as proof of the sagacity of his own caricature. For any of his readers who might have been left wondering whether this was an entirely satisfactory way of dealing with the matter, Bagehot gave them some back-up arguments. First,

The present argument breaks completely with this tradition. We contend that received opinion not only distorts the character and content of an actual Ricardian politics, but that it has also been responsible for the transmission of an image of Ricardo that is at odds with real historical figure. This is not to deny that Ricardo was recruited to the ranks of the philosophical radicals by James Mill, or that he was the party's leading spokesman on economic affairs—and this, in a quite literal sense, during his term in the House of Commons from 1819 until his premature death in 1823 as the member for Portarlington (an Irish pocket borough). Nor is it to deny the constant encouragement and editorial advice James Mill gave to Ricardo in almost all of his endeavours. However, we do wish to claim that Ricardo formulated much of what is characteristic of the democratic political creed of early philosophical radicalism in a distinctive way, that he linked his economic and political speculations in a systematic and novel fashion, and that a re-examination of the grounds upon which he made those arguments is a useful and necessary exercise in historical and theoretical recovery.

The loss incurred by too strict an adherence to the received opinion about Ricardo is not intangible. At a number of points, it would seem, the existing presuppositions about Ricardo stand in marked contrast to the opinions entertained about his significance to British political life by his contemporaries in the two decades leading up to the Reform Bill of 1832. Indeed, armed only with its caricatures, one might well be left quite bewildered as to how it was that a doctrine which was known (and opposed more regularly than supported) as Ricardianism came to occupy such a pivotal position in public discourse (one, it would seem, no less significant than that associated with the name of Malthus) at this decisive historical moment for British society.

At his death in 1823, political friend and foe alike could agree

---

stockbroking was, or so he claimed, a very abstract and unworldly vocation in any case. To clinch this point he recounted a little story (the equal of any told by Harriet Martineau or Millicent Garrett Fawcett) of a broker making thousands of pounds in railway stock without knowing where the railway actually was. Second, Ricardo was supposedly prone to abstraction as a matter of personal temperament. To clinch this point, Bagehot invoked Ricardo's Jewish origin and 'the preparation of race' (*Economic Studies*, pp. 166–68; the anti-Semitic element in these remarks will be returned to in chapter 4 below).

on at least one thing about Ricardo: his impact in the House of Commons. Brougham (for the Whigs) observed that few men had 'had more weight in Parliament', adding that 'certainly none who, finding but a very small body of his fellow-members to agree with his leading opinions, . . . ever commanded a more favourable hearing'.[9] On the floor of the House in February 1824, Joseph Hume (for the Radicals) lamented 'the extent of the loss the country had thus sustained';[10] and William Huskisson rose (for the Tories) to second. Lord Grenville considered Ricardo's death to be a 'great loss both to the country and to the Government'.[11] These establishment figures could agree on something else about Ricardo's politics, too; namely, his impeccable (though, for most of them, far too extreme) credentials as a radical in matters of politics.

But if the establishment felt that Ricardo was a little too radical for their tastes, another significant sector of the British population, the readers of the twopenny press, held him in a different regard altogether.[12] Ricardo's political influence and opinions on economic policy were well-enough known to have made him an object of frequent attack (and the butt of ridicule) in Cobbett's *Political Register*. As early as 1809, the *Political Register* had spoken disdainfully of 'the philosopher who writes for the Chronicle' when commenting upon Ricardo's very first (anonymous) contribution to the debate over wartime inflation.[13] On the occasion of Robert Peel's act for the resumption of specie payments in 1819, Cobbett's vehicle declared: 'Faith! [the economists] are now becoming *everything*. Baring assists at the Congress of Sovereigns, and Ricardo regulates things at home'.[14] The full measure of this resent-

---

[9] *Works and Correspondence* 5:xxxiv.

[10] Quoted in ibid., p. 332.

[11] From a letter to Lord Liverpool, quoted in Barry Gordon, *Ricardo in Parliament*, p. 201n.9.

[12] Samuel Bamford's remark (in *Passages from the Life of a Radical*), that Cobbett was 'read on nearly every cottage hearth in the manufacturing districts of South Lancashire, in those of Leicester, Derby, and Nottingham; also in many of the Scottish manufacturing towns' (2:12), helps to give an impression of the extent and character of Cobbett's popular audience. G.D.H. Cole suggested that, at its peak, its circulation was in the vicinity of sixty thousand copies each week (*Periods and Persons*, p. 140).

[13] The text is quoted by Sraffa in Ricardo's *Works and Correspondence* 3:26n.2.

[14] Quoted by Asa Briggs, *The Age of Improvement*, p. 205n.

ment of Ricardo's influence in these circles is captured in the following extract from the *Political Register* for 20 May 1820:

> [T]he great ass, Perry, observed the other day, that, the Inquisition being at an end in Spain, *science* would take a spread in the country; for that a Spaniard might now have 'a *Blackstone* or a RICARDO in his library!' A *Ricardo*, indeed! . . . But this Perry is, at once, the most conceited coxcomb and the greatest fool in this whole kingdom. . . . 'A *Ricardo!*' the empty, pompous fool, when it has taken but a few months to shew that '*a Ricardo*' is a heap of senseless, Change-Alley jargon, put upon paper and bound up into a book; that the measure, founded upon it, must be abandoned, or will cause millions to be starved, and that it has since been proposed, even by the author himself to supplant it by a plan for paying off the Debt! 'A *Ricardo*', indeed![15]

While thus appearing as the *bête noir* in the 'twopenny trash', Ricardo was simultaneously presented to the more reflective readers of the *Edinburgh Review* (a readership estimated by its editor Francis Jeffrey in 1814 to be around fifty thousand) as the very oracle[16] of economic wisdom. Between 1815 and 1820 it has been aptly said that 'everybody in England who thought at all was forced to form definite opinions on a series of very difficult economic problems'.[17] On issues of monetary policy, the public finances, foreign trade, and industry, it became virtually impossible to utter a single sentence without taking Ricardo's views into ac-

[15] Quoted by Sraffa, in Ricardo's *Works and Correspondence*, 5:40–41n.2. (The Perry here referred to was James Perry, proprietor of the *Morning Chronicle*.) It should be noted that the anti-Semitic overtones of some of these caricatures were soon made explicit by Cobbett's readers. In the editorial annotations to Ricardo's *Works and Correspondence*, Sraffa has noted that at a public meeting in Hereford in 1823 (at which Cobbett spoke) one speaker (a Reverend gentleman of the Church of England) referred to 'the Jew-jobbers of Change-alley' (9:267n.1). Cobbett's own anti-Semitism is noted and discussed by Elie Halévy in *History of the English People* 2:460. As already noted, we shall have reason to return to this matter in chapter 4 below.

[16] Henry Brougham, who seems (along with Cobbett) to have been the great inventor of Ricardian caricatures (and himself dubbed 'the boa constrictor' by Bentham), actually called Ricardo 'The Oracle' in a speech in the House of Commons in December 1818. The epithet stuck, and was taken up by Cobbett (see Sraffa's editorial annotations, *Works and Correspondence*, 5:40n.2).

[17] Graham Wallas, *Life of Francis Place*, p. 158.

count. So much so, in fact, that the development of debate on economic policy during the whole of the post–Napoleonic War period sometimes gives the appearance of having proceeded by way of a dialogue with Ricardo.

Were the direct influence of Ricardo on political life in Britain to have stopped there, it would have been substantial enough. But there remains a profound, if indirect influence, yet to be mentioned. By the middle of the 1820s, through the polemical writings of John Gray, 'Piercy Ravenstone', William Thompson, and, especially, Thomas Hodgskin (the early Ricardian Socialists as H. S. Foxwell dubbed them decades later), Ricardo had acquired a new reputation in quite unexpected political circles. Among these writers, the first working-class theorists in the modern sense, Ricardo's arguments were at once attacked as being essentially preservative of the existing political order,[18] and yet at the same time incorporated into a new theoretical discourse of working-class radicalism that was to be transmitted to the Chartists in the 1830s and, of course, ultimately to Marx.[19]

The reaction to which the propagation of this unanticipated aspect of the Ricardian legacy gave rise was nothing if not spectacular. In the 1820s this legacy contributed, though only in part, to a series of grand tournaments over the theory of value in which Samuel Bailey and Robert Torrens took up the battle against Ricardo.[20] A little later, even more strident critics of Ricardo were as quick to see the political implications of Ricardian economics as had been the early Ricardian Socialists. Indeed, they drew essentially the same lessons from Ricardo as had their socialist adversaries, and they took fright. To the extent that class conflict was integral to the Ricardian model of the economy, and to the extent

---

[18] As Hodgskin put it in a letter to Francis Place, 'I dislike Mr. Ricardo's opinions because they go to justify the present political situation of society' (*Letter to Place*, 28 May 1820, reproduced in Halévy's *Thomas Hodgskin*, p. 67).

[19] The Chartist connection is discussed by Mark Hovell in his *The Chartist Movement*, pp. 38–41. It is not without a certain irony that Bentham's demands for 'universality, equality, annuality and secrecy', to which Ricardo broadly subscribed, were later to be adopted as the cornerstone of the Six Points of the People's Charter.

[20] Of course, here the weaknesses of Ricardo's economic theory itself (together with the incoherent defence of it mounted by McCulloch and James Mill) played a vital role. On this point see, for example, Giancarlo de Vivo's *Ricardo and His Critics*.

that this was being deployed by the likes of Hodgskin to mandate a thorough-going restructuring of society rather than merely a measure of political reform, the defenders of existing civilization set themselves squarely against Ricardian economics. In the more socially querulous 1830s, armed, it would seem, with little save the conviction 'that what was socially dangerous could not possibly be true' (as Ronald Meek nicely put it),[21] a second wave of critics took up the banner against the Ricardian Socialists where it had been left by more able thinkers like Torrens, Bailey, and Malthus in the 1820s.[22] The decade of social unrest and disruption which began with the Reform Bill of 1832, was to see the name of Ricardo figure just as prominently in the daily rush of political life as it had done when he was alive. Given that the inter-planetary traveller myth had its origin in attempts by Ricardo's critics (both friendly and hostile) to gainsay his main arguments and conclusions, it should not come as a great surprise to find it wanting in accuracy.[23]

As to why this image of 'the impractical Ricardo' should have been transmitted for so long, it must be said that part of the an-

---

[21] 'The decline of Ricardian economics in England' (1950), p. 61. As to the socially dangerous character of Hodgskin's doctrines, his critic Charles Knight (in 1831) was in no doubt. He warned that although they began 'in the lecture room' where they appear 'harmless as abstract propositions', they 'end in the maddening passion, the drunken frenzy, the unappeasable tumult—the plunder, the fire, and the blood' (from *The Rights of Industry*, as quoted by Halévy in *Thomas Hodgskin*, p. 129).

[22] For example, writers like Mountifort Longfield, George Poulett Scrope, and Samuel Read, the last of whom spoke of the 'insulting and reckless doctrine' of rent promulgated by Ricardo and 'the Ricardo economists' (*Political Economy*, p. 301), and of their 'mischievous and fundamental' errors on value and distribution (p. xxix, n*).

[23] Something similar could be said of the whole of the philosophic-radical movement, most of whose members were regularly subjected to lampoon on such grounds. One may think of Bentham, who was disparaged as 'the man of system' by his opponents; or of James Mill, who Macaulay attacked in a famous essay for having failed to contribute to 'that noble science of politics'. Finally, Carlyle's strictures on the dismal scientists, and J. R. McCulloch and John Stuart Mill in particular, often evidence signs of the same charge—that reality (and higher sentiments) were ignored by the propagators of the 'pig philosophy'. 'Our favourite Philosophers', wrote Carlyle in 1829, 'have no love and no hatred; they stand among us not to do, nor to create anything, but as a sort of Logic-Mills to grind out the true causes and effects of all that is done and created' ('Signs of the times', p. 246). Of course, it is not entirely clear whether any of these criticisms adequately dispose of the arguments of their intended targets.

swer hinges upon the particular role in which Ricardo has been cast in the service of economics. What seems to have transpired is that economics has appropriated Ricardo rather more for the example he could provide, than for the actual theories he propounded. Ricardo has, in this context, been utilized as an ideal type. The representation so constructed seems to have been designed to operate on a number of levels simultaneously; and on all of them, the image of the ultra-abstract thinker has come in handy. On one level, mention of the name Ricardo is supposed to trigger the image of the pure theorist conducting himself in the best possible manner; seeking logical completeness and coherence in the way of a mathematician at work on his theorems. Here, Ricardo is exemplary of the very essence of the economic reasoning. At another level, thoughts of Ricardo are meant to conjure up that most sacred (and probably most vitiated) clause of the economists' code of practice: the careful separation between positive analysis and normative judgement. At still another level, however, mention of the name Ricardo is intended to sound a warning of just how far one can go wrong (think of the labour theory of value) when abstraction is carried too far.[24]

In one way or another, then, Brougham's caricature of Ricardo provided a very convenient visual aid for securing these ends. Of course, it is certainly true that Ricardo's style of reasoning has about it a Euclidian air.[25] No one who has read more than a sentence or two of Ricardo could fail to discern it. Nor were the members of the House of Commons for very long left in any doubt about it. In a speech delivered towards the end of his first year in the House of Commons on a petition from London merchants for an inquiry into the causes of commercial distress (the mover of which had claimed, not entirely without justification, that the de-

[24] It is interesting to observe that those who have mobilized the customary Ricardo-image to this salutary end, so as to highlight the dangers of the 'Ricardian Vice' of applying the conclusions of the most abstract and unreal of models directly to reality, have chosen never to mention what is probably the best example of it to be found in the whole corpus of Ricardo's work; namely, the quantity theory of money. An exception seems to be David Laidler in his entry 'Bullionist controversy' for *The New Palgrave* (1:291).

[25] James Mill was to argue, when he mustered arguments from Ricardo's *Principles* in the context of disputing the alleged benefits of a protected colonial trade, that 'there is not a proposition in Euclid, of which the links are more indissoluble' (*Colony*, p. 268).

flationary measures associated with the resumption of specie payments had much to do with it), Ricardo diagnosed the problem as being due to an outflow of capital consequent upon the existence of higher profit rates abroad, and he self-confidently reminded the House that 'no proposition in Euclid was clearer than this'.[26] But it would be mistaken to draw from this debating point the inference that his political arguments, any more than his economic arguments, were pure thought-constructs or abstract models without any direct relevance or applicability to immediate reality. The key to the understanding of this is manifest in the form and substance of Ricardo's intellectual style. It is not necessary to rehearse all that is known about Ricardo's method to grasp its essential ingredients; his extensive exchanges with Malthus exemplify it.

From these it is perfectly evident that Ricardo systematically adopted two complementary strategies when responding to Malthus's criticisms. One involved him in attempts to demolish his opponent's argument by indicating its logical inadequacies; perhaps a not too difficult task in the case of Malthus, who, as George Stigler once remarked, 'could not construct a theory that was consistent either with itself or with the facts of the world'.[27] The other involved him in a series of attempts to strengthen his own argument by incorporating those of his critics' points which seemed to compromise his conclusions (here his efforts met with more limited success). However, Ricardo's intention was not simply to seize the theoretical high ground. Though this was certainly one of his goals, just as important was the requirement of bringing to bear the arguments of political economy on the practical questions of the day. Keynes's well-known remark that when it comes to the application of economics, we should 'be lost in the wood' without 'formal principles of thought'[28] to guide us, could not better capture Ricardo's practice. To put it another way, it was issues pertaining to economic theory as a whole, as well as to its application to particular practical problems of the day, that were invariably uppermost in Ricardo's mind in his disputes with Malthus. Thus, while Ricardo could freely concede to Malthus that 'one great

[26] *Speeches and Evidence*, 19 December 1819, in *Works and Correspondence* 5:38. See also *Letter to McCulloch*, 18 June 1821, 8:390, for another allusion to the geometrical character of certain propositions in economic theory.

[27] 'Sraffa's Ricardo', p. 311.

[28] *General Theory*, p. 297.

cause of our difference of opinion . . . is that you have always in your mind the immediate and temporary effects of particular changes—whereas I . . . fix my whole attention on the permanent state of things which will result from them', this was not because Ricardo felt these short-run problems to be unimportant; for, as Ricardo continued, 'to manage the subject quite right they should be carefully distinguished and mentioned, and the due effects ascribed to each'.[29]

Needless to say, Ricardo's relentless application of these tactics against Malthus was to yield up, in the end, the desired outcome. Although Keynes would later lament that '[i]f only Malthus, instead of Ricardo, had been the parent stem from which nineteenth-century economics proceeded',[30] economics would have been the better for it, this development could hardly be said to have been the consequence of a victory of some sort of Ricardian 'empty formalism' over his friend's more subtle and measured arguments. For, on the contrary, it was the more subtle and measured arguments of Ricardo that carried the day over the confused and inconsistent ones of Malthus; and while Keynesians may still find very good grounds to rue the consequences, those grounds will have nothing to do with any alleged flaw in Ricardo's methodology.

Ricardo adopted an exactly analogous procedure in the case of politics. In the first place, when engaged in political argument, he invariably took on political thinking as a whole, and not just its discrete application to existing political arrangements. Moreover, when participatory democracy was the issue (as it is throughout Ricardo's extensive but largely overlooked writings on politics), he sought both to dismantle the logic of the argument of his critics and to make a case *in principle* for its superiority over other forms of political organization—a case which met, at least to his satisfaction, the objections raised by his detractors.

To his close friend and adversary on economic questions, Malthus, corresponded another close friend and adversary on political questions, Hutches Trower.[31] Although it would be a misrepresen-

---

[29] *Letter to Malthus*, 24 January 1817, 7:120.

[30] 'Robert Malthus: 1766–1835', in *Essays in Biography*, p. 120.

[31] Hutches Trower (1777–1833) was, like Ricardo, a member of the London Stock Exchange. They had become acquainted through their business 'in the early years of the century' (Sraffa's editorial notes, *Works and Correspondence*

tation to claim a status for the Trower-Ricardo correspondence on politics quite as grand as that Keynes claimed for the parallel Ricardo-Malthus correspondence (namely, that it was 'the most important literary correspondence in the whole development of Political Economy'[32]), it is nonetheless the case that these exchanges were instrumental in the development of Ricardo's political thought. They are typical of Ricardo's habit of developing his ideas in the context of his 'professional' correspondence, and they culminated in his writing the two discourses on politics, *Observations on Parliamentary Reform* and *Defence of the Plan of Voting by Ballot*—in much the same way as his prior correspondence with Malthus had led up to the writing of the *Essay on Profits* in 1815.

Of course, as to the relationship between Ricardo's economic theory and his political philosophy, the temptation might still remain to view it in a wholly traditional way—where the economic analysis serves as guide to good legislation.[33] But in the case of Ricardo the temptation must be resisted. That Ricardo saw the science of political economy as providing a rational foundation for the legislative deliberations of politicians cannot for a moment be doubted.[34] His service on seven select committees during his par-

---

6:xxiii), and 'discovered' themselves to be 'great admirer[s] of the work of Adam Smith, and of the early articles on Political Economy which had appeared in the Edinburgh Review' (*Letter to Trower*, 26 January 1818, 7:246). In 1813, 1814, and 1815, Trower (like Ricardo) had been among the successful bidders for government loan contracts (see *Works and Correspondence*, vol. 10, 'Table: Loans for Great Britain and Ireland, 1805–1820', pp. 80–81). Sraffa notes that 'Trower has no claim to literary fame in his own right; he is only remembered because of this correspondence' (*Works and Correspondence* 6:xxii). However, given the importance of this correspondence to the formation of Ricardo's political thought, it is somewhat surprising that all Sraffa has to say about it in his editorial apparatus is that its 'peculiar interest' lies in the example it provides of 'an attempt to explain to a comparative layman the economic discussions in which Ricardo was engaged' (*Works and Correspondence*, 6:xiv).

[32] *Essays in Biography*, p. 114.

[33] Thus, D. P. O'Brien's argument that, for the classical economists, '[e]conomics is seen as providing the statesman's guide to economic growth' (*The Classical Economists*, p. 34). The effect of this tradition on the accuracy of historical reconstructions of the work of these theorists should not be underestimated. It has led to a situation where the argument that for the classical economists 'forms of government were largely immaterial' (as one recent writer has put it; Claeys, *Citizens and Saints*, p. 144) is allowed to pass without comment or query.

[34] This sentiment was clearly articulated by Ricardo to Robert Torrens in 1818

liamentary term, his prominent involvement in public debates over the Bullion Report (1810) and the Corn Laws (1815), his expert evidence before parliamentary committees on the Usury Laws (1818) and the resumption of specie payments (1819), together with his proposal for the nationalization of the Bank of England, only attest to that fact. To be sure, Ricardo's contribution to the status which economists today seem to enjoy as expert advisers should not be underestimated. Nevertheless, to the extent that this picture of the economist-as-adviser dates back (at least) to Adam Smith, in advocating and even embodying it, Ricardo hardly ·stands apart from a general tendency that seems to have been at work within classical economics.[35] In this arena, his was just another contribution (albeit an important one) to an existing conception of the relation between economics and politics; one which has long been entertained by practicing economists.

But this is not at all what is distinctive and significant about Ricardian politics. What sets Ricardian politics apart, what makes Ricardo more than just another economic adviser, is what he has to contribute to democratic theory proper. Furthermore, in the hands of Ricardo, economic theory itself had something to contribute to the strictly political question of the organization of the polity as well. It is precisely this dual contribution to politics by Ricardo which represents the neglected strand in the political thought of the philosophical radicals that we wish to rescue from oblivion.

(Torrens was standing in the general election for the seat of Rochester): '[F]rom your knowledge of Political Economy, your advice would be of essential use in all financial questions, and at present there appears to be a great dearth of that sort of talent amongst our legislators' (*Letter to Torrens*, 15 June 1818, 11:xii). As it transpired, Torrens failed to be elected in 1818 (and, although returned for Ipswich in 1826, he was subsequently disqualified after the success of a petition challenging his election). Torrens finally succeeded in his ambition to enter parliament in 1831 when he was returned for Ashburton. At the general election for the reformed parliament in 1832 he was returned for Bolton. Torrens retired from the House of Commons in 1835.

[35] This statement should not be taken to discount the added impetus given to this tendency by the programmatic goals of the philosophic-radical movement itself. Quite apart from James Mill's recruitment of Ricardo to the cause (for what seems to have been this very purpose), one may think of the recruitment of the young Edwin Chadwick, whose subsequent professional activities were to have such far-reaching effects in rationalizing the administrative apparatus of government (see, for example, S. E. Finer: *The Life and Times of Sir Edwin Chadwick*, especially chaps. 2 & 3).

Ricardian politics, we shall argue, is in an important sense richer and more expansive in both of these departments than that of the other philosophical radicals. Its political philosophy, *per se*, has little affinity to Bentham's politics, which (as others have observed) often sound so much like those of the 'man of system' singled out for disapprobation by Adam Smith. Nor, despite the many assertions to the contrary by subsequent commentators, does it bear the characteristic imprint of James Mill; whose arguments often resemble nothing so much as those of the lawyer rather than the philosopher.[36] Even when measured against John Stuart Mill, who alone among the philosophical radicals is usually said to have avoided the shortcomings of both Bentham and his father, Ricardian politics comes off well.

In the first place, unlike his philosophic-radical friends, Bentham and James Mill, Ricardo was in a better position to harness the science of political economy to the science of politics, if only because neither Bentham nor James Mill could seriously be described as having been in command of a theoretically informed version of economic science. Bentham's *Manual of Political Economy*, for example, though not published during his lifetime, is not a systematic treatise on the subject (or, for that matter, even an unsystematic treatise) but a set of stage directions instructing politicians on their lines ('Be Quiet') and where to stand ('out of my sunshine').[37] James Mill's *Elements of Political Economy*, compiled (it seems) from the reports that his teenage son was required to write up after Mill had lectured to him on Ricardo during their walks together,[38] and intended as a school textbook, was sufficiently muddled as to get wrong two of Ricardo's key theoretical propositions (on the modifications to the theory of value and the effects of machinery).[39]

[36] Elie Halévy makes just this observation in his *Philosophic Radicalism*, p. 421.

[37] *Manual of Political Economy*, as printed in Bowring's edition of Bentham's *Works*, 3:35. With a little more generosity, some might say, Stark described the *Manual* as a '*catalogue raisonné* . . . of the measures at the disposal of government' in his edition of Bentham's *Economic Writings* (1:49).

[38] See John Stuart Mill's *Autobiography*, p. 19.

[39] Ricardo himself pointed these errors out to Mill (*Letter to Mill*, 18 December 1821, 9:127), but no reply from Mill is extant—and the revisions he made to subsequent editions (after Ricardo's death) only made matters worse. A full discussion of their significance can be found in Giancarlo De Vivo's *Ricardo and His*

Furthermore, by structuring his thinking about politics around an account of the operation of the market mechanism in this way, Ricardo's political thought was not, formally speaking, utilitarian. That is to say, unlike Bentham and James Mill, whose thinking about politics was exclusively grounded upon a strict application of the utilitarian model of human nature, Ricardo grounded his upon a model of economic functioning. Casually speaking, of course, since he certainly conceived the end of government to be the 'greatest happiness' of the nation, Ricardo could be said to have been a 'utilitarian' (of sorts). The problem is that on such a casual definition scarcely anyone would not have been utilitarian; a fact James Mill (stepping down from the philosophical heights) sometimes deployed to disarm his critics.[40] However, as we shall endeavour to show, this apparent agreement masks quite deep differences in both the content and mode of analysis Ricardo applied in arriving at a design for political society that might secure that end.

To summarize, then, we shall endeavour to establish three basic claims about Ricardian politics.

First, that Ricardo developed a systematic and democratic platform which drew at key points on, as he called it, the science of political economy. We shall spell out in some detail the manner in which Ricardo drew this connection between democratic theory and political economy. It should be said quite plainly that this part of our argument challenges not only the idea that Ricardo had no substantive political thought at all, but it also serves to attach an important rider to the opinion that he was an uncritical 'prop of

---

Critics, pp. 19–24. The harshest judgement on James Mill's performance came from Marx who claimed that 'the *disintegration* of the Ricardian school "therefore" begins with him' (*Theories of Surplus Value* 3:84). Donald Winch, writing in *The New Palgrave*, records that Mill 'bowdlerized the theory' (3:466). A more sympathetic picture of Mill was painted by Eric Stokes in his *Utilitarians and India* where James Mill is referred to as 'an expert on political economy' (p. 81).

[40] Thus, in his *Fragment on Mackintosh*, we find that 'the whole of Plato's Republic may be regarded as a development, and, in many parts, a masterly development, of the principle applied by Mr. Mill' (p. 285). Apart from Plato, Bishop Berkeley and Blackstone are also mentioned. On this score, James Mill was only to be outdone by his son, who added Jesus of Nazareth to the list: 'In the golden rule of Jesus of Nazareth we read the complete spirit of the ethics of utility' (*Utilitarianism*, p. 32).

the middle classes'.[41] Furthermore, we hope to be able to demonstrate that Ricardo's economics, which the majority of commentators on philosophical radicalism seem to find so enigmatic, is integral to his democratic politics in a way more subtle than that implied by the view that economic theory simply provided a rational template through which to pass judgement upon the various economic policies favoured from time to time by practising politicians. For Ricardo, economic theory was not just a useful adjunct to the science of the legislator (as Adam Smith intimated in a famous passage), it was integral to the science of politics itself.

Second, we shall provide evidence that Ricardo reached his own conclusions independently, and indeed before, the publication of James Mill's essay on *Government* (1820) for the Supplement to the *Encyclopedia Britannica*; an essay which according to received wisdom was supposed to have provided Ricardo with his politics. This should give the lie to the idea that Ricardo is best understood as having been scripted and stage-managed by James Mill in matters political.

Finally, we shall show that Ricardo developed a quite sophisticated argument for democratic citizenship as a pre-requisite for economic progress. This argument, though it bears many of the characteristic features of co-optation arguments, seems at once to be more modern and more resilient than many of the arguments advanced by other philosophical radicals of the time whose names are accorded rather more status in the canon of political thought than that of Ricardo.[42]

---

[41] Arnold Toynbee, *The Industrial Revolution*, p. 127.

[42] 'Could it be', as Thomas De Quincey once said of Ricardo's achievements as an economist, 'that an Englishman, and he not in academic bowers, but oppressed by mercantile and senatorial cares, had accomplished what all the universities of Europe, and a century of thought, had failed even to advance by one hair's-breadth?' (Thomas De Quincey, *Confessions of an English Opium-Eater*, p. 255).

Representative Government

In DECEMBER 1819, in the debate on the second reading of one of the Six Acts passed in reaction to events at Peterloo in the preceding August, Lord Palmerston (then Secretary of War) rose from the Ministerial benches of the House of Commons to defend his earlier action in signing a counter-requisition against an application to convene a public meeting in the county of Hampshire. He had acted, he said, 'from a well-understood sense of duty', and in so doing, he went on to claim, he 'had consulted the best interests of the country',[1] by which he meant his own perception of what those interests were. In his few brief remarks on that occasion, Palmerston gave a simple and unambiguous rendering of much that was characteristic of the existing system of representation in Great Britain, and of the substance of the theory of representation that lay behind it.

The system was not equal. The 658 members of the House of Commons were returned at septennial general elections by an all-male electoral body amounting to scarcely more than 2.5 percent of the entire population.[2] The political voice of the disenfranchised was heard, when it was heard at all, only at a suitable distance. Their right to petition the Crown had been granted under a Bill of Rights that dated back to the reign of William and Mary.[3] The system was not uniform. The House of Commons comprised county, borough, and university representatives. County representatives were returned on a franchise which extended to the celebrated forty-shilling freeholder. The English counties returned

---

[1] *Hansard*, 41, c.676.

[2] Estimates of the size of the electorate in 1831 can be found in Halévy, *History of the English People*, 3:27n.5, and Flora, *State, Economy, and Society*, 1:149.

[3] 'That it be the right of the subjects to petition the King and all commitments and prosecutions for such petitioning are illegal' (Bill of Rights, 1689, reproduced in Adams and Stevens, *Select Documents*, p. 464). The Riot Act of 1714, of course, significantly curtailed this legislative provision which in any case countenanced the legality of large public gatherings *only* for the purpose of petitioning—not for general expressions of public outrage.

two members, while their Scottish and Welsh counterparts returned only one. Borough representatives were returned on a startlingly heterogeneous franchise. It ranged in character from that of the potwalloping and scot-and-lot boroughs, at one end of the spectrum, through the corporation boroughs, right down to that of the rotten and pocket boroughs, at the other. The old universities of Oxford and Cambridge each sent two representatives to Westminster, and Trinity College, Dublin, sent one. The great majority of English boroughs sent two members to Westminster (although two of them returned four), while a handful returned just one.[4] The system was subject to abuse. Votes were traded, seats were traded, and patronage ruled the roost. George III apparently earmarked £12,000 at general elections to secure the election of candidates with Ministerial support. The Treasury and the Admiralty were also players in the market, seeking to swell the Ministerial benches.[5] In 1812 the Duke of Bedford sold the entire borough of Camelford, with nine electors, for £32,000.[6] Fi-

[4] For a summary of the character of selected electoral districts, see Cook and Stevenson, *British Historical Facts: 1760–1830*, p. 47 et seq. A more substantive account of the system of representation is given by Halévy in his *History of the English People*, 1:115 et seq. The standard authorities on the subject are T. H. B. Oldfield's, *Representative History* and Edward Porritt's, *The Unreformed House of Commons*.

[5] To take just one example, Dartmouth was a government borough with forty voters of which Oldfield remarked that 'the treasury and the admiralty having the nomination of the members . . . the farce of electing might as well be performed by clerks in those offices, as at such a distance from London' (*Representative History* 3:341–42).

[6] See Oldfield's *Representative History*, 3:236 (a transaction which, it might be noted, deprived Henry Brougham of his seat). Ricardo himself was returned for Portarlington (Ireland) in consideration for a loan of £25,000 (at 6 percent) and a payment of £4,000 to Lord Portarlington. According to Halévy, Portarlington was one of eighteen Irish boroughs 'where the franchise belonged to a close corporation, twelve burgesses chosen by co-optation . . . [in] these cases the right to elect the member was the private property of the landlord, who had succeeded in making himself the "patron" of the corporation' (*History of the English People*, 1:119 & n.1). Not that the radical reformers thought that this was all bad. James Mill, for example, wrote in 1827 that the 'men who most frequently open their way to Parliament by the direct instead of the indirect use of the purse, are men of mercantile wealth'; and he enquired rhetorically of existing representatives: 'Are they a class of men whom their country has less cause to trust than it has to trust you?' ('Constitutional legislation', p. 342). One should also recall Bentham's famous remark that if he had £10m or £20m he would 'buy liberty with it for the people' (*Plan of Parliamentary Reform*, 3:486).

nally, although Lord Liverpool is reported to have said in 1810 that he regarded this 'theoretic inequality' as 'one of the greatest advantages of our constitution',[7] the system had come under siege from the people.

In consulting only himself as to the best interests of the nation on all occasions, Palmerston openly stamped himself as a representative of the old kind. A representative, or so it was claimed, whose elevated character and ability had won him his office. He was a lawgiver, not just someone's deputy; his was a notion of representation that did not entertain for a moment what de Tocqueville once called (betraying, perhaps, his aristocratic leanings) the 'theory of equality applied to brains'.[8] A representative, or so it was claimed, whose sense of duty required the sternest forbearance in the face of temptations that might divert him from his honour-bound and virtuous path (like the temporary popularity he might enjoy consequent upon actually consulting the mass of the people, rather than himself, on legislative matters). Not for him the paths of narrow-mindedness, or of self-interest, or of unbridled lust for power; for him, politics was a vocation (quite literally so, since it was unpaid). In short, a representative of a species which the swelling wave of democracy that was to envelop Britain over the next one hundred years or so would thankfully render extinct.

It was against the theoretical and practical foundations of this system of representation that the early philosophical radicals waged their celebrated and lengthy campaign for parliamentary reform. It was in the context of this campaign that David Ricardo was to make his most distinctive contribution to the science of politics.

Although Ricardo had discussed politics with James Mill as early as 1815,[9] his thoughts on the subject of representative government were formulated in the last three-quarters of 1818; the period immediately preceding his taking up a seat in the House of Commons in 1819 as the member for Portarlington.[10] They were developed

---

[7] Cited in R. J. White, *Waterloo to Peterloo*, p. 68; and this from the man who Brougham claimed 'was never known to utter a word at which anyone could take exception' (*Historical Sketches* 2:121).

[8] *Democracy in America*, p. 247.

[9] See *Letter to Mill*, 30 August 1815, 6:262–64; and *Letter to Mill*, 24 October 1815, 6:311.

[10] Ricardo's 'commonplace books', though not extensive, contain evidence of

in an extensive correspondence with Hutches Trower, less extensive exchanges with James Mill and Malthus, and in the two discourses on politics written towards the end of 1818 and published posthumously in 1824.[11] This intense period of writing and formulating political argument was a relatively quiet time for Ricardo the economist; he had finished the first edition of his *Principles* early in 1817 and wrote nothing new until his article on the *Funding System* in 1820 for the Supplement to the *Encyclopedia Britannica*. That it happened also to correspond to a period during which political events in the country took a dramatic turn, and to the period during which the negotiations surrounding Ricardo's entry into parliament were taking place,[12] cannot have been incidental to its timing.

Of course, the rapidity with which Ricardo developed his thinking about politics was nothing if not spectacular. Nevertheless, the performance was quite in keeping with his earlier track record in economics. Ricardo had developed what was, up to that time, one of the most sophisticated presentations and applications of the quantity theory of money in the space of a little over twelve months (namely, those immediately preceding, and those that followed, the printing of the Bullion Report in August 1810).[13] If one

---

this formal turn to politics. Of the sixty pages identified as belonging to 1818 (and summarized by Sraffa in *Works and Correspondence* 10:394–98), the entries are entirely on politics (where Fox's speeches figure prominently) and religion.

[11] This fact, which became known with the publication of the relevant volumes of the definitive edition of Ricardo's *Works and Correspondence* in 1952, may help to explain why earlier commentators had not taken Ricardo's politics very seriously. It does not explain why, in the thirty-five years since, no attempt has been made to revise the received opinion (see, for example, Hamburger's remarks in *Intellectuals in Politics*, pp. 7–8). It should also be noted that Ricardo wrote a paper on reform in 1819, but it has been lost (see editorial annotations to *Works and Correspondence* 8:6n.1).

[12] For an account of how this came about, see Sraffa's editorial introduction to the fifth volume of *Works and Correspondence* (5:xiii–xvii). The event immediately precipitating the plan (long advocated by James Mill) was the departure (on medical advice) of Francis Horner for Italy in 1816 (who later died at Pisa in 1817).

[13] Ricardo had entered the Bullion Controversy with an anonymous article 'The Price of Gold' which appeared in the *Morning Chronicle* for 29 August 1809. He then participated (signing his letters 'R') in the lively correspondence to which the article gave rise (one of his anonymous critics turned out to be Hutches Trower; they carried on the debate in private once they had discovered each

leaves out of the account the name of Henry Thornton, there was simply no exponent of the quantity theory of money whose contribution could even approach in quality that of Ricardo. The entire Ricardian theory of distribution, perhaps his most significant contribution to classical economic theory, was constructed in the eighteen months that led up to the publication of the *Essay on Profits* in February 1815.[14] To this not insignificant achievement he added, during the first ten months of 1816, the whole of the theory of value which eventually appeared as the first chapter of his *Principles* in April 1817.[15]

Nor did Ricardo allow his limited, if not non-existent, political education stand in his way. In connection with 'the Parliamentary scheme', as he called it, he requested James Mill to provide him with a reading list: '[t]ell me however what to undertake and I will put my powers to the test'.[16] Mill recommended (along with his own *History of British India*) Locke (the *Essay*), Hume, and John Millar.[17] To this list Ricardo added Bayle, Burke, Thomas Reid, Dugald Stewart, and Montesquieu, remarking of the latter's *Espirit des lois* that he expected 'to see something better on that subject by and by'.[18] Nor was this remark intended as a glib dismissal. Ricardo went on to add his own specific reservations about elements of Montesquieu's political design, and these suggested not only a serious engagement of the merits of the argument but also that independent, critical stance which appears to be the hallmark of Ricardo's thinking about politics.[19] But this is not the typical way in which Ricardo's politics have been construed.

---

other's identity). Early in January of 1810 the *High Price of Bullion* was published, and by December of that year his *Reply to Bosanquet* was at the printer.

[14] The actual text of the *Essay on Profits* itself was written in just a few days. See Sraffa's editorial annotations in *Works and Correspondence*, 4:4–5.

[15] The first sign of Ricardo's turning his attention to the theory of value was 30 December 1815; by 14 October 1816, he had dispatched the draft of the first seven chapters of the *Principles* to James Mill (see Sraffa's editorial annotations in *Works and Correspondence*, 1:xiv–xv).

[16] *Letter to Mill*, 12 September 1817, 7:190.

[17] *Letter to Ricardo*, 19 October 1817, 7:197.

[18] *Letter to Mill*, 28 December 1818, 7:383.

[19] Ricardo added the following by way of critique: 'His views are liberal but he speaks too much in favour of Glory and of pure Monarchy,—and the virtue which he makes the active principle in Republics is represented too much as a disinterested principle of action' (7:383).

It is customarily suggested that Ricardo sided with the Opposition in support of a moderate reform of parliament principally because it seemed to him to be the 'most efficacious preventative to Revolution'.[20] Indeed, like many a commentator on British constitutional arrangements, both before and after him, Ricardo drew on the case of Ireland to exemplify this point:

> If Catholic emancipation and a reform in Parliament had been granted to the Irish at the time that Lord Fitzwilliam was Lord Lieutenant would there have been a Rebellion in Ireland?[21]

What is less frequently attended to in this 1819 remark to James Mill, however, is Ricardo's more expansive, democratic claim that not only could political reform be 'at all times safely conceded',[22] but also that most of the challenges faced by government arose from its stubborn refusal to *listen* and to take seriously the legitimate demands of the people. As Ricardo saw it, the legitimacy of public demands seems to have rested on the sheer numbers of those making such demands: 'the people themselves, through the means of their representatives, should have a preponderating voice'.[23] The failure of government to listen was the direct consequence both of its undemocratic character and of the broader set of constitutional arrangements upon which it was grounded.[24] In

[20] This would seem to be the general sentiment behind the remarks on the subject in the entry on David Ricardo in *The New Palgrave* 3:184.

[21] *Letter to Mill*, 10 August 1819, 8:50. Ricardo was speaking of the 2d Earl Fitzwilliam who had been sent as Lord-Lieutenant to Ireland by Pitt in December 1794, and who was dismissed in March of the following year for what the Cabinet saw as his overly accommodating attitude towards Catholic claims. Interestingly enough, Lord Fitzwilliam's liberal sentiments were to bring him down again in 1819, when he was removed from the Lord-Lieutenancy of the West Riding for taking the chair at a public meeting in York called to press for an official inquiry into the events at Peterloo.

[22] *Letter to Mill*, 10 August 1819, 8:49.

[23] *Letter to Trower*, 18 September 1818, 7:299.

[24] It is worth remembering that the Tory government of the day was of a heterogeneous character. It had its 'ultras' and its more 'liberal' factions. Even among the liberal Tories, however, the position on reform of the existing constitutional arrangements remained narrow. George Canning, on the liberal wing, seems to exemplify this view. In a speech at the conclusion of the poll at Liverpool in 1818 he opened by remarking that he believed that 'the historian of future times will be at a loss to imagine how it should happen, that, at this particular period, . . . there should arise a sect of philosophers in this country, who begin

Ricardo's opinion, these problematic arrangements were the result of subscribing to an outmoded and woefully inadequate theory of virtual representation. It was these arrangements which Ricardo argued ought to be changed, not just as a preventative to revolution, but on principle. And it was in the name of this principle that Ricardo called for the reform of a House of Commons 'in which not one sixth of the representatives are chosen by Ireland'.[25]

This older theory of virtual representation, articulated by many, but perhaps never more effectively than by Edmund Burke at the end of the eighteenth century, maintained that members of parliament were entrusted to represent 'virtually' the interests of their constituents (identified as the good of the nation), rather than to represent directly their immediate and discrete interests (or the interests of various powerful societal factions within the nation). On Burke's understanding, '[v]irtual representation is that in which there is a communion of interests, and a sympathy in feelings and desires between those who act in the name of any description of people, and the people in whose name they act, though the trustees are not actually chosen by them'.[26] Burke contrasted this theory of representation favourably with 'actual' rep-

---

to suspect something rotten in the British constitution' (*Memoirs* 3:275). He went on to declare that the whole object of his political life had always been 'to reconcile the nation to the lot which had fallen to them' (p. 279).

[25] *Letter to Trower*, 10 August 1819, 8:50. This call very clearly established Ricardo's credentials as a radical reformer. Whig reformers never went this far. Lord John Russell, for example, in his speech on the disenfranchisement of Grampound, set out that position with a memorable turn of phrase: 'The principles of the construction of this House are pure and worthy. If we should endeavour to change them altogether we should commit the folly of the servant in the story of Aladdin, who is deceived by the cry of "New lamps for old". Our lamp is covered with dirt and rubbish but it has a magical power. It has raised up a smiling land. . . . And, sir, shall we change an instrument which has produced effects so wonderful for a burnished and tinsel article of modern manufacture? No. Small as the remaining treasure of the Constitution is, I cannot consent to overthrow it into the wheel for the chance of obtaining a prize in the lottery of constitutions' (quoted in Spencer Walpole's *Life of Lord John Russell* 1:108n.1). Brougham, in 1827, revealed his opinion of the radicals; they were 'a set of drivellers who call themselves a kind of *doctrinaires*, and hold opinions subversive of all liberty, as that the minister is never to be blamed, but only the system' (*Letter to Lord Landsdowne*, 26 March 1827, quoted in Arthur Aspinall's *Lord Brougham and the Whig Party*, p. 145).

[26] *Letter to Sir Hercules Langrishe*, 3 January 1792, *Works* 3:521.

25

resentation (a view he saw most closely attuned to the constituent demands of revolutionary American colonials) and which he called a 'confused and scuffling bustle of local agency'.[27] However, to obtain the objectivity and independence of judgement necessary to discern the communion of interests required by the Burkean model of virtual representation, an elected representative had to assume the heroic task of ignoring (and even in some instances actually opposing) constituent and public opinion on legislative matters. 'Your representative owes you, not his industry only, but his judgement; and he betrays, instead of serving you, if he sacrifices it to your opinion'.[28]

Behind this heroic role for the legislator, then, lay a more or less well-developed argument as to the general incapacity of the electorate (and the nation-at-large) for involvement in genuine self-government, understood as 'matters of reason and judgement'.[29] Specifically, it entailed a claim as to the inability of the public to distance themselves from immediate or pecuniary advantage.[30] On this line of thinking, the public was seen as less than wholly rational, ruled by momentary passions; as 'a sort of children that must be soothed and managed'.[31] The only possible result of a more directly democratic polity, so the argument ran, was a struggle in the political arena between discordant narrow interests; and this to the eternal detriment of the nation. The Burkean model of government by virtual representation is one of an evolved balance of powers, among basically harmonious (organic) components of the nation, achieved through the wise and virtuous direction of matters of state by representatives. It is, very obviously, a view that links present politics inextricably with the past through the traditional accretion of good government. At the same time, of course, it portrays the 'machinery of government' as being safe in the hands of knowledgeable and virtuous mechanics.

These various parts of Burke's political vision—the infantile public, the representative as mechanic and hero, and representative office as both a vocation and honorific prize demanding objec-

[27] *Speech at Bristol Previous to the Election* (1780), in *Works* 2:238.
[28] *Speech at Bristol at the Conclusion of the Poll* (1774), in *Works* 2:12. See also the discussions at pp. 87–135, 233–89 (especially pp. 236–37).
[29] Burke, *Works* 2:12.
[30] Ibid., pp. 236, 237, 240, 242, 264, 279.
[31] *Speech at Bristol Previous to the Election* (1780), in *Works* 2:279.

tivity and self-sacrifice[32]—comprised a rationale for simultaneously excluding large numbers from the electorate, and for ignoring the demands of constituents in calculating the common good. However, as a profound critic of 'visionary' schemes of government, Burke himself was well aware that the ideal of virtual representation was not always consonant with parliamentary practice and that decision-making within the House of Commons was often based less on 'reason and judgement' than on victories in a struggle of passions and interests.[33] Burke was not resistant to the need for political change and reform. Nevertheless, Burke's basic understanding of the nature of man, together with his theory of political power, led him to refuse to enlarge the political nation or to open up the franchise to include anything more than, for instance, the virtual representation of Catholics in Ireland.

By the turn of the century, Whig reformers were seeking a platform for greater, though still moderate, parliamentary reform within the strictures of the Burkean tradition of virtual representation. In the pages of the *Edinburgh Review*, philosophic Whig reformers like James Mackintosh and Francis Jeffrey attempted to unseat the standard impression of the Whig perspective as being essentially aristocratic in character, and thus practically indistinguishable in terms of political principle from that of the Tories.[34] Of course, the need for a restatement of Whig principles was made all the more urgent by their electoral failures, as well as by the challenge they faced from a small yet vocal group of radicals for the mantle of genuine parliamentary opposition and reform. Thus, Whig reformers sought to re-address the question of 'what mode of representation is most likely to secure the liberty, and consequently the happiness, of a community circumstanced like the people of Great Britain',[35] in light of the increasingly apparent fact

[32] Burke, *Works* 2:254–59.

[33] Ibid., pp. 18, 255–56.

[34] In his standard account, *Lord Brougham and the Whig Party*, Arthur Aspinall has quoted Sir Walter Scott as suggesting that the only difference between a Whig and Tory lay not in principle—'there is and can be none'—but rather in 'words and personal predilections' (p. 41). More to the point, Aspinall also notes that their broad similarity actually led Hazlitt to remark that the two parties 'reminded him of rival stage coaches which bespattered each other with mud, but which travelled along the same road and arrived at the same destination' (p. 41).

[35] James Mackintosh, 'Universal suffrage', p. 174.

that the 'political public' had become 'not only far more numerous, but more intelligent, more ardent, more bold, and more active'.[36] Both Mackintosh and Jeffrey perceived the extent to which such developments in the political nation posed a potential threat to public liberty and that great object of Government—'security against wrong'.[37] Their answer was virtual representation restated.[38]

On this view, even a reformed representation must remain firmly tied to locale and to the great orders—'all districts and communities'—which comprised society—not to individual constituents:[39]

[36] Ibid., p. 172.

[37] Ibid., pp. 174, 183; Francis Jeffery, 'State of the country', pp. 296, 299. Jeffrey argued that the chief impetus to civil disturbance was the failure of government to secure the existing rights of subjects who, on other grounds, might be 'very fit' for exclusion from the elective franchise.

[38] Mackintosh, 'Parliamentary reform', pp. 475–77 and Jeffrey, 'State of the country', p. 299. Mackintosh's position seems particularly important in encapsulating what will be referred to elsewhere in this study as the 'new virtualism'—of both the Whig reformers' attitude toward franchise reform, and that of certain Radicals such as James Mill. In brief, Mackintosh argued that '[i]f we were compelled to confine all elective influence to one order, we must indeed rest it in the middling classes. . . . It is right that they should have a preponderating influence, because they are likely to make the best choice' ('Universal suffrage', p. 191). Yet, at the same time, unlike Mill and the radicals, Mackintosh was unwilling to disregard or challenge the claim of the 'higher classes' to influence the direction of parliamentary policy, since he believed them to be more capable than the middling class of resisting the temptations of Government (read Ministerial) influence and favouritism and more likely to display a Burkean independence which only a 'commanding wealth' makes possible. This unwillingness sprang precisely from his older conception of virtual representation, which in Fox's terms, 'calls into activity the greatest number of independent votes, and excludes those whose condition takes from them the powers of deliberation' (p. 192). The overarching Whig commitment to the principle of independence likewise determined Mackintosh's rejection of the secret ballot. First, the ballot would not remain secret—the 'zeal, attachment and enthusiasm' of elections mitigates against it. Second, if secrecy were successfully adopted, 'it would, in practice, contract, instead of extending, the elective franchise, by abating, if not extinguishing, the strongest inducements to its exercise'. '[W]here votes are secret, scarcely any motive for voting is left to the majority of electors' (p. 195). Mackintosh's argument against the secret ballot, that it will deprive electors of their 'public spirit' and reason for voting, which is acquiring favortism—'to gain the favour of his superiors', 'the kindness of his fellows', and the gratitude of the candidate for whom he votes'—is precisely the opposite of the motivation which he supposes should guide representatives when they vote (pp. 195, 198).

[39] Mackintosh, 'Parliamentary reform', p. 475. Mackintosh took pains to sug-

The Representative assembly must therefore contain,—some members peculiarly qualified for discussions of the Constitution and the Laws, others for those of Foreign Policy;—some for the respective interests of Agriculture, Commerce, and Manufactures;—some for Military affairs by sea and land, and some also who are conversant with the colonies and distant possessions of a great empire.[40]

Reform, on this model, would be understood to extend the elective franchise to some of the 'laborious classes'[41] on two distinguishable grounds: utility, in that it 'betters the character, raises the spirit, and enhances the consequence of all', and bestows 'a hold on the estimation of their superiors'; and justice, in that 'nobody has ever observed that there is in England a . . . difference between the husbandman and the mechanic—who have votes, and who have not'.[42] On the whole, however, pragmatism rather than vaunted political principle seems to have been the determinant of the extent of reform. As Mackintosh himself claimed, '[T]he exclusion of the [labouring] class degrades the whole; but the admission of a part bestows on the whole a sense of importance, and a hold on the estimation of their superiors'.[43] Moderate Whig reformers such as Mackintosh and Jeffrey thus remained firm in their attachments to the essentially Burkean view that 'most men imbibe prejudices with their knowledge' which should have no place in the legislature's deliberation of 'laws conducive to the well-being of the whole community',[44] and that this was true to an even greater degree with regard to labourers. Therefore, with regard to representation, they concluded that 'the best chance for an approach to right decision, lies in an appeal to the largest body of well-educated men, of leisure, large property, temperate character, and who are impartial on more subjects than any other class of men'.[45] The preponderant share of reformed legislative influence should thus fall to the 'middling classes', though not by dent of numbers

---

gest that such a reform fit within the nation's ancestral 'principle', 'that every great community, with distinct interests, ought to have separate representatives' (p. 475).

[40] Mackintosh, 'Universal suffrage', p. 175.

[41] Ibid., p. 172.

[42] Ibid., p. 183.

[43] Ibid.

[44] Ibid., p. 175.

[45] Ibid., p. 176.

but 'because they possess the largest share of sense and virtue, and because they have the most numerous connexions of interest with the other parts of society'.[46] The tendency of such a middling class to employ their political influence in the pursuit of Ministerial favours would, it was argued, be balanced in parliament by the steady and 'independent' guidance of their 'higher leaders' in the wealthy upper classes, and balanced outside parliament by the periodic demands 'and even turbulence of their inferiors' in the still disenfranchised lower classes. In this fashion, these Whig reformers chose to guide political reform by reversion to what Mackintosh termed the 'ancient standard' of 'steady and disinterested principles'[47]—the model of balanced orders—which included both the public vote and the virtual representative.[48]

For Ricardo, on the other hand, writing almost simultaneously with the outpourings of the *Edinburgh Review*, virtual representation was the obstacle, not the answer, to franchise reform. Indeed, though he wrote some twenty years after Burke's last reflections on the Irish question, Ricardo explicitly raised that question again in order to argue that it was the theory of virtual representation itself which effectively justified the Irish demand for independence. On Ricardo's argument, that theory had ensured that 'the interests of England will prevail in all cases where they may happen to clash with those of Ireland. Is there any remedy against this but independence? Do you think that a representative Government is more or less disposed to tyrannise over its distant unrepresented possessions than a pure Aristocracy or Monarchy?'[49] Nevertheless, the essential ingredients of the Burkean position (albeit revised and restated by moderate Whig reformers) on virtual

---

[46] Ibid., p. 191. Mackintosh's sentiments, shared by others like Jeffrey (and even Radicals such as James Mill), indicates an earlier date for the entrenchment of the phrase 'middle class' as a political concept than has been suggested by Asa Briggs. (See 'Middle-class consciousness in English politics', p. 65.) As Briggs himself notes, by 1831 Brougham was prepared to make the following equation: 'By the People, I mean the middle classes, the wealth and intelligence of the country, the glory of the British name' (p. 69, citing Brougham from *Hansard* 8:c.251).

[47] Mackintosh, 'Universal suffrage', p. 170.

[48] Ibid., p. 177.

[49] *Letter to Mill*, 10 August 1819, 8:50. For Burke's thoughts on the Irish question in 1792, see *Letter to Sir Hercules Langrishe*, 3 January 1792, in *Works* 3:481–531.

representation was still being defended in 1818, by figures such as Mackintosh and Jeffrey, and with greater strains evident in the seams of the argument.[50] It was a view defended even within the circle of Ricardo's friends, as the correspondence between Hutches Trower and Ricardo provides a case in point. The correspondence with Trower particularly helps to set apart and illuminate Ricardo's own distinctive views on representative government when contrasted with those of these moderate Whig reformers.

In an exchange of letters with Ricardo in late 1818, Trower defended the position of virtual representation and public voting against Ricardo's arguments for reform.[51] The essential ingredients of Trower's defence echoed the Burkean assumption that 'experiment and experience, the perfection of all things' had worked to produce Britain's present mixed and balanced constitution, which was in no need of general reform.[52] Instead, Trower recommended that 'conflicting sentiments should be *quietly* arranged by means of influences moderately operating', and that the 'ultimate result of the deliberations of the Legislature, should be the *mixed and mellowed opinions of the three branches*'.[53] Politics, thus personalized, was for Trower a matter not of general rules but of the 'feeling and observation' of Burkean statesmen, whose duty it was to 'bear constantly in mind, that the Government, over which he presides, is a complicated piece of machinery, . . . it is his imperious duty to endeavor, at all times, to *preserve the balance*'.[54] For politics in general, the implications of this characterization of government was that participation must be restricted, and that even the right of voting at elections ought to be confined 'to such persons,

[50] Thomas Perronet Thompson passed harsh judgement on the virtual representationists: 'Noah was a prodigious radical, when, hearing the world was to be drowned, he went about such a commonsense proceeding as making himself a ship to swim in. A Whig would have layed half a dozen sticks together for an ark and called it a virtual representation' ('Radical reform', p. 228).

[51] The exchange between Ricardo and Trower over various political topics is extensive between 1816 and 1818 and is contained in *Works and Correspondence* 7:11–13, 15–18, 21–23, 33–35, 44–51, 62–65, 94–97, 116–19, 266–68, 272–75, 287–90, 308–11, 318–24, 340–46.

[52] *Letter from Trower*, 24 November 1818, 7:343.

[53] Ibid., italics in original.

[54] Ibid., p. 344.

who by their education have the ability to decide correctly; and who by their situation have the power of deciding correctly'.[55]

While Trower's machine metaphors suggested the need for the special expertise of representatives who combined 'wisdom and virtue' to tinker with the balance of powers as needed, he himself noted that there was at the time a real 'dearth of talent'[56] among the representatives in Parliament. He recognized as well 'there should be an effectual check on the Government, in the people'.[57] However, consistent with his Burkean position, Trower believed that the unreformed House of Commons as it stood provided for such a check, and that there was a greater need to control the growth of public opinion than to incorporate it through enfranchisement:

> The force of public opinion *is*, and *must be* felt in Parliament; and that the rapid and inevitable growth of that opinion makes it a much more important consideration how the influence of that opinion should be properly regulated, than how it should be increased.[58]

What is interesting about Trower's opinion is that, on first glance, it registers less a fear of popular political capacity than a fear of *any* political change at all.[59] After all, Trower does speak of 'wealth, knowledge and independent spirit' as 'spreading rapidly among the people'. But the 'natural tendency' of this improvement in capability, for Trower, threatened to 'give too much force to the popular part of our Constitution, to render it *too republican*'.[60] Trower did not deny that improvements in the political performance of the existing governmental arrangements were necessary; but he would not reform government for fear of fouling the 'mix'.[61] At bottom, Trower's principal fear was the overthrow of the monarchy, an outcome which he saw as a necessary consequence of representing too wide a range of popular opinion; a force which he held to be largely irrational and 'which when let loose or politically

---

[55] Ibid., p. 342.
[56] Ibid., 7 June 1818, 7:267.
[57] Ibid., 23 August 1818, 7:289.
[58] Ibid., p. 290; italics in original.
[59] *Letter to Ricardo*, 23 August 1818, 7:290.
[60] Ibid.; italics in original.
[61] See, for example, *Letter from Trower*, 18 October 1818, 7:309–10.

empowered would be incalculable in its objects, and irresistible in its effects'.[62]

Trower's more positive position on any increase in the practical force of popular opinion—a development which seemed to reflect, in his mind, advances in capability rather than a hightened misery index—was that it should be felt 'without', or rather outside of the constitution, in the traditional form of irregular and vocal popular protestations, rather than being felt routinely 'within' the government by an increased or more inclusive representation. The latter he felt was bound to upset 'mixed government'. Ricardo, of course, was only too quick to recognize that Trower's fears of the irresistibly revolutionary tendencies of the popular order had little basis in experience (except in the ghost of France) and easily elided with Trower's other claims about its advancing knowledge and personal independence.[63] If anything, Ricardo implicitly recognized the lack of reason (namely, logic) in Trower's own position: it assumed an irrational stance in claiming that only a mixed government was legitimate, on the argument that even if it was not working, it could be made to work (where 'work' simply meant good government as 'well-ordered'; and 'well-ordered' was understood as a mixed government in which decisions of the public good were removed from the people and the representatives were assumed to hold a special position of privileged knowledge and capacity). As Ricardo noticed, much to his own amusement, Trower had not actually proven that only a mixed government was legitimate, but rather that only a mixed government was mixed.

Ricardo's view of good government differed significantly from Trower's. It was developed not only in their correspondence, but also in the two discourses on parliamentary reform which Ricardo wrote during 1818, prior to his own election to parliament, but

[62] Ibid., p. 310.

[63] Ricardo was always at pains to debunk the argument that reform would open the door to anarchy and that the unenfranchised represent a revolutionary threat. He found support for this view in radical circles of his day; Francis Place (himself an exemplar of the rational tradesman) popularly espoused this idea (see his *Autobiography*, p. 130). What is interesting, however, is that among the classical economists, Ricardo's view seems to have been exceptionally democratic. (Compare McCulloch in 'The British cotton manufacture', pp. 37–38; McCulloch's position is discussed in more detail by Coats in 'The classical economists and the labourer', p. 155.)

which were only published posthumously. On Ricardo's view, the representative's function was cast neither in heroic nor virtuous terms. Ricardo expressed a general distrust of any idea of virtue which was too far removed from self-interest and happiness. On Ricardo's understanding, government was not a matter of mechanically balancing the powers; he used no machine metaphors which would purport to require of representatives great mechanical talents. Accordingly, Ricardo expressed greater optimism about the character and direction of public opinion.[64] Indeed, Ricardo framed his response to Trower's defense of an unreformed and virtually representative House of Commons in terms of enlarging the existing view of the 'reasonable part of the country'.[65] For Ricardo, the franchise could safely be extended to 'all *reasonable men*' who had no *sinister* or *particular interest* opposed to the general interest, who harboured no presuppositions about the value of government in and of itself, and who could show themselves capable (literally) of following a logical argument.[66]

Ricardo's political language comprised a re-evaluation of the common man's ability to reason about matters touching on the public good. In his letters to Trower, he repeatedly referred to the opinions of 'reasonable people' in order to argue for the validity and responsibility of judgements made by those to whom the elective franchise had not yet been extended. He accused Trower of not 'trusting' reasonable men to choose between a mixed government and a republic, on the straightforward grounds that Trower had assumed that 'reasonable people' were 'so besotted that they will give up a greater good for a smaller' and thus would eliminate the monarchy even if they saw it as important to good government.[67] Ricardo's reply to this claim offered a humourous but sardonic analogy that suggested Trower had no 'adequate motive' or evidence for such a judgement:

> Men have the power, which is almost uncontroulable, of destroying themselves, but we confine them in straight waistcoats only when we discover that they think they have adequate motives for employing this power to their own destruction.[68]

[64] See, for example, *Letter to Trower*, 2 November 1818, 7:320.
[65] Ibid.
[66] Ibid., pp. 320–21.
[67] Ibid., p. 321.
[68] Ibid., pp. 321–22.

Ricardo insisted, rather, that it was not enough simply to assert that the 'popular part of the constitution would become irresistible' under franchise reform. Trower had to show that it was a bad thing that this should be so. At other points in their correspondence, Ricardo made the stronger argument that 'public opinion . . . ought [to control] in all governments whose end, and object, is the happiness of the people'.[69] Unlike Trower, Ricardo chose to identify public opinion with the opinions of reasonable men whose judgements could be trusted. Moreover, he took the more radical step of arguing that public opinion ought to control the government and that the actions of representatives should conform to constituents' demands. He substituted the utilitarian terms 'happiness of the people' for the virtual representative's 'top-down' references to the 'public good'; and he legitimated the popular preference for republics over monarchy in such terms:

If a republic be the best form of government, and will best promote the happiness of the people, we must not *quarrel with reform for its tendency to give us a republican government*.[70]

For his part, Trower accused Ricardo of a certain amount of idealism in choosing to place political faith ultimately in men rather than in the 'perfection' of the machinery of a mixed and balanced constitutional monarchy. On Trower's argument, Ricardo had effectively created a mixed constitution in name and a republic in form.[71] Ricardo deflected this accusation with a few sobering observations of his own, pointedly maintaining that the 'balanced constitution' was a chimerical argument for doing nothing.[72] (James Mill ironically characterized it by that most dismissive of eighteenth-century epithets, 'visionary'.[73]) The mechanical metaphors of virtual representation simply obfuscated the central tensions between the present structure of government and its purported ends. According to Ricardo, there was no 'balance' in the constitution as it existed, nor could there ever be. While it was true that the monarchy 'would not long venture to oppose the opinion decidedly expressed by the House of Commons' who ef-

[69] Ibid., p. 322.
[70] Ibid., p. 320; italics added.
[71] See, for example, *Letter from Trower*, 24 November 1818, 7:341, 344.
[72] See *Economists*, p. 721.
[73] See *Government*, p. 15.

fectively decide 'all great questions' of the nation, nevertheless Ricardo noted the Commons failed to provide an adequate check on either the Monarchy or the Lords. The 'House of Commons is not appointed by the people, but by the Peers and the wealthy aristocracy of the country'.[74] Effectively, this meant that 'all the power and influence which Government gives' was 'divided' in a 'compromise between the aristocracy and the monarchy'.[75] Without another, more viable check on power, England's government would be no better, Ricardo argued, than 'despotic'.[76] However, a check of sorts did exist. Ricardo observed that 'the check is not in the constitution—it is as I said before in public opinion, expressed through the medium of the press—in trial by jury—in the published speeches of a few popular members of parliament, who have no influence by their votes, but by their tongues, and in the right of convening public meetings and thereby organizing opposition— these are the checks to which we owe all the happiness and liberty we enjoy'.[77] But Ricardo surmized 'that a regular reliance on aroused popular opposition to government action recognized to be hurtful to the interest of the nation was as unreliable as it was unsystematic'.[78] Thus the 'ideal of government' would more likely be achieved if the people themselves were directly and frequently consulted through an enlarged franchise:

> Of all the classes in the community the people only are interested in being well-governed; on this point there can be no dispute or mistake. . . . A reform in the House of Commons then, the extension of the elective franchise to all those against whom no plausible reason can be urged that they have, or supposed they have, interest contrary to the general interest, is the only measure which will secure liberty and good government on a solid and permanent foundation.

[74] *Parliamentary Reform*, 5:495. Indeed, at no point in the hundred years preceding the Reform Bill of 1832 did the House of Commons consist of less than one-third of its members whose social rank was connected directly to the peerage. See Judd, *Members of Parliament*, Appendix 6, p. 84.

[75] *Parliamentary Reform*, 5:496.

[76] Ibid. 'If, then, there were no other check . . . England would not have to boast of a better Government than that what exists in those countries in which it is called despotic'.

[77] *Letter to Trower*, 20 December 1818, 7:368.

[78] *Parliamentary Reform*, 5:496.

This is so self-evident that one is surprised that an argument can be offered against it.[79]

On this reasoning, Ricardo thus proposed as an immediate reform of parliament the expansion of the elective franchise just short of universal suffrage. He expressed confidence that with the rapid increase in 'knowledge and intelligence' afforded by this initial reform, 'in a limited space of time . . . we might, with utmost safety, extend the right of voting for members of Parliament to every class of the people'.[80]

At the centre of his *Observations on Parliamentary Reform*, as well as the contemporaneous Trower-Ricardo correspondence, are found those precise conflicts over the character of political change and choice that ultimately separated the premises of an older, aristocratic politics from that of an emerging and modern democratic theory: conflicts over the character of social and political change; over the stability and advancing competence of common men to rule themselves; over the general estimation of 'the people' who make up the political nation; and centrally, over the relationship of the perceived and politically directed interest of the labouring classes to that of the nation-at-large.

For his part, Ricardo did not fear political change, which in any event he saw as both inevitable and necessary. Later, he would deny in language reminiscent of Jefferson (and the French *Ideologues* whom Jefferson mimicked), that 'the present generation ought to be bound down by all that had been done by their ancestors', suggesting instead that the claims of tradition require legitimating arguments beyond itself.[81] Indeed, if the monarchy could not be justified in terms of the 'happiness of the community', then Ricardo would be satisfied to see it fall in the present generation.[82] From Ricardo's perspective, Trower's 'illogical' attachment to the maintenance of the 'balanced constitution' was simply an argument for doing nothing, an alternative all the more unappealing, since

[79] Ibid., pp. 498–99.

[80] Ibid., pp. 502–3.

[81] *Speeches and Evidence*, 20 February 1823, 5:283.

[82] *Letter to Mill*, 28 December 1818, 7:381. In his speech supporting Lord John Russell's motion for a reform of parliament, Ricardo suggested that should a reformed House of Commons 'propose to dismiss the Crown and the House of Lords, it would be because they were unnecessary to the good government of the country' (*Speeches and Evidence*, 24 April 1823, 5:286).

Trower too recognized (indeed, feared) the 'inevitable', progressive change in the social character and capabilities of the unenfranchised public. For Ricardo, the argument that a reform proposition might be recognized as beneficial and yet rejected as 'not the constitution under which we were born', was a mischievous argument capable of being 'used to perpetuate every abuse and every evil.'[83] The refusal to alter the governmental 'balance' so as to adapt to inevitable social changes (or worse, to use the Lords as a tool to 'check' such changes) Ricardo perceived as not only a futile effort but a position courting political disaster: it was to make revolution all but necessary.

The distance separating Ricardo and Trower on the expanded franchise and general political change reflects the difference between their respective estimation of both the nascent stability and rational faculties of common men. Trower seemed to think that the more they knew, the more disruptive the common people would become, and on this apparent reasoning supported measures such as the Six Acts which restricted the right of popular meetings and public petitioning of the Government for the removal of grievances.[84] Ricardo, on the other hand, opposed such measures as being on their face 'serious infringements of liberties'.[85]

It is worth emphasizing that the specific liberty at issue, for Ricardo, was not simply 'the right of the people to petition' the government, but rather their right to do so in numbers sufficient to 'afford a hope that bad measures would be abandoned'.[86] In this instance, as on other issues, Ricardo recognized the actual capability as well as the principled right of the people to recognize and demand the correction of 'bad' governmental policies. Ricardo chose to defend this putative right to efficacious public assembly on the explicit argument that while such a check ought not to exist in a 'well-administered government', under the existing political arrangements it was the people's only check against despotism.

Far better, Ricardo reiterated in his attack on the Six Acts, to dissolve the need for such public petitionings by reforming the franchise and transforming the petitioners into voters. His defense

[83] *Speeches and Evidence*, 24 April 1823, 5:287.

[84] Ricardo, at least, was convinced he supported them. *Letter to Trower*, 28 December 1819, 8:146.

[85] Ibid.

[86] *Speeches and Evidence*, 6 December 1819, 5:28.

of both activities rested on what he perceived to be a relationship between advancing knowledge (that is, progress) and stability, and on what he took to be the increased evidence that common people were capable of forming clear opinions of their own interests,[87] which on grounds of either political pragmatism or justice could not legitimately be ignored. Indeed, he argued that it was precisely because '[t]he people at large now possessed so much more information than they ever before possessed, that they were entitled to be better represented in parliament than they had ever been before'.[88] His willingness to treat equally the claims for knowledge and judgement of the people against those of any particular government, was grounded upon his belief (which he articulated to James Mill well in advance of the latter's own essay on *Government* for the Supplement to the *Encyclopedia Britannica*) that 'in the progress of knowledge the people became more sensible of the fences necessary for their security'[89] and were prepared to use them as a guide to politics.

For Ricardo, the question of reform moved beyond the extension of the suffrage to two other considerations which he believed to be, if anything, of 'deeper interest': the mode of election and the duration of parliaments. In both his parliamentary response to the 1823 motion of Lord John Russell for a reform of parliament and his earlier *Defence of the Plan of Voting by Ballot*, Ricardo argued against the wisdom and indeed the legality of the existing open-vote system of election. His arguments for the importance of the secret ballot complement and extend those he developed against Trower in defence of both general franchise reform and, in particular, the direct representation of Irish Catholics. The elective franchise should be extended in order to counterpose the disproportionate numerical influence of the English aristocracy, and likewise a mode of secret balloting must be substituted in order to free existing and newly enfranchised voters from the undue influence of the more economically powerful classes.[90] His effort was to attack the premises underlying a system of election in which 'votes

---

[87] *Letter to Mill*, 28 December 1818, 7:380. As to why Ricardo thought that the people had attained this capacity for political decision-making, the reader may consult chapter 3 below.

[88] *Speeches and Evidence*, 24 April 1823, 5:287.

[89] *Letter to Mill*, 28 December 1818, 7:380.

[90] *Speeches and Evidence*, 18 April 1821, 5:112.

are more effectually secured by the fear of loss than by the hope of gain'.[91] From Ricardo's perspective, the defence of the open-vote system (as with the defence of virtual representation) sprang from the same outdated vision of the political world. It was, after all, Burke who had argued that '[a]ll contrivances by ballot, we know experimentally to be vain and childish to prevent the discovery of inclinations. Where they may the best answer the purposes of concealment, they answer to produce suspicion, and this is a still more mischievous cause of partiality'.[92]

In Burke's characterization of the virtuous political community, all must know where each stands, otherwise distrust infects the relationship between rulers and ruled. At the same time, of course, Burke presumably recognized the window of opportunity opened to the occasional dishonourable landlord to corrupt the open-vote system so as to serve his own advantage. But in the case of virtual representation, what was seen by Burke (and with more justification than by Trower) to be simply unfortunate and occasional lapses in an otherwise preferred method of distributing political power, Ricardo characterized as the systemic instrument through which a single, landlord class—that class whose interest was, as Ricardo put it, necessarily opposed to the interest of every other class in the community—was permitted to perpetuate its political hegemony.[93]

> It is the most cruel mockery to tell a man he may vote for A or B, when you know that he is so much under the influence of A, or the friends of A, that his voting for B would be attended with the destruction of him. . . . Is it not a delusion to say that every freeholder of 40s. a year has a vote for a member of parliament, when in most cases he cannot vote as he pleases, without ruin to himself? It is not

[91] *Defence of the Ballot*, 5:507.

[92] Burke, *Works*, 3:238. It is worth noting that not all those in favour of democratic reform also supported the ballot. Percy Bysshe Shelley, for example, was set against it (see *A Philosophical View of Reform* 7:44).

[93] *Principles*, 1:335. See Ricardo's disagreement with Malthus in his *Notes on Malthus*, 2:116–17. While Ricardo denied that he perceived landlords as 'enemies of the state', he recognized that their interests in maintaining an artificially high price for corn did run counter to the interests of all others and was a power which they continually exercised in parliament. There is a further discussion of this matter in chapter 5 below (see also Collini, Winch, and Burrow, *That Noble Science of Politics*, pp. 73–74 and Donald Winch's *Malthus*, p. 101).

he who has the vote, really and substantially, but his landlord; for it is for his benefit and interest, that it is exercised in the present system.[94]

We have already noted the fact that in his response to the parliamentary motion of Lord John Russell, Ricardo had argued that such a system of open voting was 'illegal'; and it will repay the effort to pause for a moment to examine just what this curious-sounding claim actually meant. Since open voting followed parliamentary prescription, Ricardo can only be understood to mean that depriving citizens of the 'free exercise' of a right already secured to them by law violates natural fairness or justice (as well as the laws of logic) and as such was, *de facto* if not *de jure*, unconstitutional. He dismissed the argument that if left to choose in secret, the people would be incapable of selecting men of sufficient talent with a brief allusion to Montesquieu:

> Could we doubt that natural capacity of the people to discern real merit, it would only be necessary to cast our eyes upon the continued series of surprising elections which were made by the Athenians and the Romans, which undoubtedly no one could contribute to hazard. It is well known that although at Rome the people possessed the right of electing the plebians to public offices, they never chose to exercise that power; and although at Athens, by the law of Aristides, they were allowed to select the magistrates from every rank of the state, yet the common people, says Xenophon, never petitioned for such employment as could possibly interfere with their safety and glory.[95]

One is left to wonder whether Ricardo seriously considered that an argument for deferring to the plebian practices of either the Romans or the Greeks could be expected to carry much weight with those of his contemporaries opposed to the secret ballot. The more so, since he understood well that no argument would carry weight, because the opposition to the secret ballot was not grounded in rational argument: 'I have never heard any solid reasons for their objections:—they are all to be resolved to an antip-

[94] *Defence of the Ballot*, 5:506.
[95] *Speeches and Evidence*, 24 April 1823, 5:289, citing Montesquieu, *Espirit des lois*, Livre 2, chap. 2.

athy, for which they can give no account.'[96] Against prejudice, neither logic nor reasons could be expected to register. As for Ricardo himself, however, it simply strengthened his confidence that the people, even prior to more recent advances in knowledge, could be expected to act as 'wisely and prudently' as those presently enfranchised, if left to an 'unrestricted exercise of their choice'.[97]

What all of this renders transparent, is the hitherto neglected fact that Ricardo's theory of representation conveyed the core of a modern, direct representation in which the wisdom and judgement of the people was identified with their ability to ascertain their own best interests and to rely on the pursuit of that interest (and public happiness) rather than the virtue of their representatives as the truest political compass in arriving at the public good. In this more radical vision, the importance of issues and interests to some extent supplants the political importance of particular individuals. A more general representation was therefore needed in Ricardo's vision in order to reflect accurately the interests and issues of importance to public happiness, rather than to realize any abstract demand for individual natural rights. It is in this sense that Ricardo understands the holders of political power in terms of classes, rather than individuals, and in this manner that he substitutes the idea of classes and class interests for the more traditional Whig view of individuals as the key actors in politics.[98] This difference helps to distinguish and highlight the novelty of Ricardo's political thinking not only from the Whigs but also from some of the philosophical radicals with whom his name has previously been most closely linked. Indeed, exemplary of this is the contrast between Ricardo's theory and that particular strand of philosophical radicalism typified by James Mill.

As is well known, Ricardo spoke and corresponded extensively with James Mill on both theoretical and practical issues of politics

[96] *Letter to Trower*, 18 September 1818, 7:299.

[97] *Speeches and Evidence*, 24 April 1823, 5:289.

[98] It is important to recognize that Ricardo believed individuals knew very well their own interests and used them (rather than virtue) to guide politics, but he conceived of these interests in larger, class terms rather than in the liberal individualist sense of strictly private interest. This conception of class interest is especially evident in Ricardo's famous dictum that 'the interest of the landlord is necessarily opposed to the interest of every other class in the community' (*Notes on Malthus*, 2:116–17).

from 1817 until Ricardo's death in 1823.[99] During that time, the elder Mill encouraged Ricardo to write down all his thoughts on politics, and especially to record those which would later be contained in the two discourses on politics, 'with the purpose', Mill wrote, 'of sending them to me'.[100] Despite Mill's encouragement, and indeed his cultivation of Ricardo's development as a political thinker (and parliamentarian), the political writings of the economist very quickly moved beyond the conceptual categories and principles of his mentor. Perhaps most obviously, Ricardo's political thought is not strictly utilitarian and indeed he made explicit arguments challenging Mill's own use of utility as a standard against which to measure justice and well-being.[101]

Yet Ricardo's vision of politics differed from Mill's in other equally decisive ways. Here the contrast is between a fundamentally individualistic conception of political action and one based, as it was for Ricardo, on class interest. Mill's focus on the importance of theorizing about the individual political actor led him to assert that 'the whole science of human nature must be explored, to lay a foundation for the science of politics'.[102] Ricardo neither required nor sanctioned such an extensive and potentially controversial groundwork to isolate the shortcomings of representative politics as it then operated in Britain.[103] More important, Mill's view of human nature was of an essentially aggressive and domineering pleasure seeker who, if unchecked, will 'as a law of human nature . . . take from others anything which they have and he desires.'[104] This view ran counter to Ricardo's explicit observations about what one could rationally assume to be the motivations for human and social action.

[99] Although Ricardo first met Mill in 1808, and had become his close friend by 1810, it seems they did not engage in any serious discussion of politics until Ricardo's return from the continent after the publication of the *Principles* in 1817.

[100] *Letter from Mill*, 23 September 1818, 7:302. See also *Letter from Mill*, 24 August 1817, 7:183.

[101] *Letter to Mill*, 6 January 1818, 7:242. For the developed discussion of Ricardo's own standard of well-being, and for a discussion of the reasons for his rejection of one based on utility, see chapters 3 and 4 below.

[102] *Government*, p. 3.

[103] And as it was to turn out, *actually* controversial. This very grounding provided Macaulay with an excuse for attacking Mill some ten years later for giving 'too much weight to some of the motives to human action, and too little to others' ('Mill on politics', p. 236).

[104] *Government*, p. 8.

It was on the presumption that 'there is no limit to the number of men whose actions we desire to have conformable to our will',[105] that Mill based his arguments for both the actual need and the necessary structure of government:

All the difficult questions of Government relate to the means of restraining those, in whose hands are lodged the powers necessary for the protection of all, from making bad use of it. Whatever would be the temptations under which individuals would lie, if there was no Government, to take the objects of desire from others weaker than themselves, under the same temptations the members of the Government lie, to take the objects of desire from the members of the community, if they are not prevented from doing so.[106]

This view of a political world in which power must constantly check power led Mill to reject in principle the three 'pure forms' of government—democracy (the many), aristocracy (the few), and monarchy (the one), or any theory of a combined or 'balanced' government of all three. No set of powers so aggressively construed could possibly be expected to compromise.

The Democracy or the Community have all possible motives to endeavour to prevent the Monarchy and Aristocracy from exercising power, or obtaining the wealth of the community, for their own advantage: The Monarchy and Aristocracy have all possible motives for endeavoring to obtain unlimited power over the persons and property of the community: The consequence is inevitable; that have all possible motives for combining to obtain that power, and unless the people have power enough to be a match for both, they have no protection.[107]

It is on the basis of this 'demonstration', and the corollary that any interest not shared by (that is, not identical with) the community was a 'sinister interest', that Mill extrapolated his theory of representative government.[108] In achieving representative government, the 'real object to be aimed at in the composition of the legislature', Mill argued, 'is to prevent the predominence of the interest of any individual or of any class; because if such interest

[105] Ibid., p. 11.
[106] Ibid., p. 5.
[107] Ibid., p. 16.
[108] Ibid., p. 19.

predominates . . . it will be promoted at the expense of the community'.[109] The only form of government which would check the tendency of the Monarchy or the Aristocracy to domineer was one which places the power of government (identified as the legitimate power to check) in the community. However, the people themselves (Democracy) could not be trusted actually to exercise these powers, therefore they must be handed over to a 'body of men, called Representatives'.[110] But how were these representatives themselves to be prevented from domineering? Mill's answer was twofold: through brief (unspecified) terms of office and, more important, through limiting and shaping the character of the *electors* eligible to choose such representatives to ones whose interest can be ascertained to be identical to that of the community.[111] The mechanisms for this second and most important political task were the secret ballot and public education.

In the *Parliamentary Review* of legislative activity during the sessions of 1826–1827 and 1827–1828, Mill contributed a review essay on 'Constitutional legislation' in which he argued that the existing system of open voting promoted the corruption of politics in at least two ways. First, it obviously enhanced the ability of the rich to give a veneer of electoral legitimacy to their own sinister interests by exerting pressure on those beneath them to cast votes in their support: 'if the poor man cannot conceal from the rich man how he votes, the rich man knows to a certainty when his price commands his commodity, and he can make sure of it'.[112] Second, the open system was necessarily morally corruptive of the poor, since 'the voter, whether he be a good man, or a bad man, would, if he followed his own inclination, vote differently from the mode in which influence is exerted to induce him to vote'. The consequence for the citizen, Mill argued, was that if 'he is a bad man, and disregards a promise, he votes as he pleases, knowing he may do so with impunity; and his promise passes for nothing. If on the contrary we suppose that he is a good man, the good man knows that it is a bad thing to make a bad promise; but a worse thing to

[109] James Mill, 'The seventh Imperial Parliament', p. 781 (see Hamburger's *Art of Revolution*, p. 22).

[110] *Government*, p. 18.

[111] Mill's commitment to frequent (if not annual) parliaments will be discussed below in chapter 6.

[112] 'Constitutional legislation', p. 365.

keep it'.[113] Either way, the virtue of the would-be voter is im-
puned. The secret ballot became in Mill's view the single most
important preventative to rule by the rich.[114] However, the secret
ballot alone could not prevent the rise of another, equally sinister
interest—that of the poor. Here Mill's answer was not to 'check'
it, but to educate it.

'The virtue of people, you say, is weak. Unhappily it is so, de-
plorably weak', Mill wrote in the July number of the *Westminster
Review* for 1830 in an essay on 'The ballot'. However, to improve
it required more than franchise or electoral reform. Thus, an indispensable component to Mill's parliamentary reform proposals
was a plan of education. The complex details of that plan are of less
importance to this discussion than is its unambiguous purpose: to
create a community of shared (common) interest out of individuals
whose interests could neither naturally nor originally be understood as coincident or bound up with that of others. When one
turns to Mill's most extensive political statement, the essay on
Government, the paramount necessity of the existence of such a
coherent moral and political 'community' in order to make his proposal for a reformed government 'representative' through the
'identity of interests between ruler and ruled' becomes clear. Referred to by Mill as an 'exposition of the Elements of Political
Knowledge', the essay on *Government* isolates middle-class morality as the most important component of political knowledge available to the masses. Consonant with his general and rather sketch-
ily crafted argument in the essay on *Education* for the Supplement
to the *Encyclopedia Britannica*, that the foundation of mental life
is grounded on associations (mental sequences), it is necessary for
political knowledge that the individual develop the correct associations or 'primary habits' of mind.[115] The appropriate habits or as-

[113] Ibid. For Mill's expanded discussion of the morally corruptive effects of the
open-vote system, see 'The ballot', pp. 8–10.

[114] 'The ballot, and that alone, can enable [the people] to choose, and render
the British constitution in reality what it now is only in pretence' ('The ballot', p.
17). Or elsewhere, with rather more rhetorical flourish, Mill wrote: 'Make voting
secret, and who will pay for a vote which is of no value, when it cannot be known?
Make voting secret, and who will incur the expense of bringing distant voters to
the poll, who may all vote for the opposite party?' ('Constitutional legislation', p.
362).

[115] The relevant passages here may be found in James Mill's article *Education*,
pp. 71–99, and especially pp. 93–96.

sociations for the laboring classes were to be formed through their assimilation of the moral norms and values of that 'virtuous and intelligent rank'; the middle rank, 'which gives to science, to art and to legislation itself, their most distinguished ornaments . . . advice and example'.[116]

In the essay on *Government*, these norms provide the foundation of the community, and enable one to identify as representatives those individuals whose interests are consonant with it. Here, the discussion of creating a genuine community of interest which can safely select representatives who convey its virtues into politics replaces any direct discussion of the radical proposals for 'universality, equality, annuality and secrecy.'[117] An ungenerous observer might even be forgiven for thinking that Mill—despite his avowal of friendship with 'the plebian, the democratical'[118]— had done little more for the theory of representation in the essay on *Government* than to invent a 'new virtualism' to replace the old. However, it is not ungenerous to claim that in thus shifting the focus of achieving 'good government' away from the virtue of the representative and placing it instead on that of the community of electors, Mill's theory of government takes at best only a dubious step toward modern representative democracy. It ensured that his approach to expanding the franchise was almost wholly negative; so much so, that when applied it proved to exclude from the franchise all but the 'aggregate males' of the community who could meet the 'indentity of interest' criterion.[119] The difficulties of ascertaining just how exclusive or expensive this theory of representation proves to be is the subject of chapter 4 below. However, it is worth noting here that while both Mill and Ricardo pro-

[116] *Government*, p. 32. Of course, not all democratic reformers had such sanguine views of the middling rank. Shelley for one, thought that they 'poison the literature of the age in which they live by requiring either the antitype of their own mediocrity in books, or such stupid and distorted and inharmonious odealisms as alone have the power to stir their torpid imaginations. Their domestic affections are feeble, and they have no others. They think of any commerce with their species but as a means, never as an end, and as a means to the basest forms of personal advantage' (*A Philosophical View of Reform*, p. 29).

[117] Indeed, as William Thomas has noted, 'At a time when moderate radicals were becoming more hesitant and popular radicals more extreme about the traditional radical demands for universal suffrage, shorter parliaments and the ballot, the *Essay* managed to evade all three' (see 'James Mill's politics', p. 257).

[118] 'The ballot', p. 6.

[119] *Government*, p. 21.

fessed a desire to see the interest of the community expressed in politics, their respective visions of this 'community' were quite different. For Mill, the community was one marked by shared, even homogeneous interest, and it existed only as an abstract ideal to be realized (constructed) in the future. For Ricardo, on the other hand, the community of general interest was the one that actually existed with its class diversity intact, but which present forms of representation failed to reflect. This difference in their articulation of the notion of community, something which appears to have been overlooked by earlier historians, may help to explain the occasional expressions of frustration by John Stuart Mill, who shared his father's hope for the construction of this ideal community of interest, at the slow progress being made toward it during his own lifetime: 'In England, it would hardly be believed to what degree all that is morally objectionable in the lowest class of the working people is nourished, if not engendered, by the low state of their understandings. . . . Few have considered how anyone who could instil into these people the commonest worldly wisdom—who could render them capable of even selfish prudential calculations—would improve their conduct in every regulation of life, and clear the soil for the growth of right feelings and worthy propensities'.[120]

In contrast to Ricardo's vision of representation, which placed a value on bringing into government the existing diversity of interests (especially class interests) present in the community, James Mill's theory stressed commonality and uniformity. Underlying this contrast is, of course, Ricardo's more profoundly optimistic understanding of the role of conflict in politics. Explicit in Ricardo's argument for the expanded franchise and the secret ballot was a belief that all 'the reasonable people' who might potentially participate in the formulation of public policy, had yet *actually* to participate in it. The question Mill had not answered in any satisfactory or modern way was who 'the reasonable people' were. This was a question which Ricardo quite self-consciously addressed, and in his answer resides an important and original contribution to democratic thinking in the early nineteenth century. It is to this matter that we now turn.

[120] 'The claims of labour', p. 511; on this point see also the discussion in A. W. Coats, 'The classical economists and the labourer', pp. 152–53.

The Reasonable Part of the Country

IF GOVERNMENT was to be constituted so as to be representative of public opinion in a directly democratic way, as Ricardo had proposed, then the question immediately arose as to the extent of the enfranchisement thereby mandated. This question was, and remained for years to come, the bane of philosophic-radical political thinking. It is what gives that characteristic flavour of elitism (and, according to some, of class bias) to the opinions of some of the most advanced liberals of the first half of the nineteenth century. John Stuart Mill was still grappling with it when he came to formulate his *Considerations on Representative Government* in 1861, an essay he later characterized as marking his own transition from a commitment to 'pure democracy' to a 'modified form of it'.[1] His well-known advocacy of plural voting and the system of proportional representation devised by Thomas Hare are only the most obvious examples of its presence.[2]

As a rule, in addressing the question of who should vote, or, what (to them) amounts to the same thing, the question of political citizenship, the philosophical radicals spoke in voices which they adjusted to suit the circumstances. At bottom, of course, it was a matter of principle and had to be dealt with as such. Bentham seems to have been the only one truly to have realised this; and he paid the price of going out on a limb with his motto "Universality, Equality, Annuality, Secrecy". But in many instances, especially in the context of actual political struggles, where there was a real possibility of securing a measure of parliamentary reform, a note of expediency regularly entered the discourse of philosophical radicalism. James Mill's essay on *Government* seems to stand as exemplary of it. Indeed, it might even be said that the elder

---

[1] *Autobiography*, p. 134.

[2] It was, of course, also John Stuart Mill's solution to his perception that keeping the pace of political change gradual was a pre-requisite to social stability. We shall have cause to return to this point in chapter 5 below, when we examine Ricardo's views on the speed of reform in more detail.

Mill never really addressed the question of enfranchisement at the level of principle at all.[3]

Ricardo was no exception to this rule. Although he did declare himself against any piecemeal approach to reform on the floor of the House of Commons in 1823, when he was faced with the charge that democracy was an avatar of the end of civilization, Ricardo spoke in an accommodating voice. Thus, one can find him talking of securing 'unbiased good sense' among electors,[4] of enfranchising only 'the reasonable part of the country',[5] of getting 'all the wisdom and virtue of the country to act in Government', and of taking 'precautions' in 'bestowing the elective franchise'.[6] As we have already mentioned, in his speech to the House of Commons on Lord Russell's motion for a reform of parliament, Ricardo even invoked the authority of Montesquieu to support his faith in 'the people' and to bolster his main conclusion 'that instead of selecting demagogues and disturbers of the peace, as was unjustly apprehended, the people, if left to the unrestricted exercise of their choice, would act wisely and prudently'.[7]

But it is one thing to have to meet the scare-mongering of political adversaries head-on in parliamentary debate (and the direct involvement of the philosophical radicals in daily politics helps to explain why they devoted so much attention to the moral character of electors in that particular context), it is quite another to settle the issue of the extent of the franchise on principle. What is decisive about Ricardo's contribution to that more theoretical project, is that he seems to have resolved the matter of principle in a way which sets him apart not only from James Mill, but also from John Stuart Mill (whose best-known intervention in the debate came some forty years after Ricardo's death). This, together with Ricardo's early re-adjustment and criticism of the notion of virtual rep-

[3] Elie Halévy went so far as to claim that Mill's case for representative government 'is the argument of a lawyer rather than of a philosopher'. *Philosophic Radicalism*, p. 421. From what has been said in the previous chapter, it will be clear that herein lies an important difference between Ricardo and Mill.

[4] *Letter to Trower*, 22 March 1818, 7:260; see also *Letter to McCulloch*, 17 January 1821, 8:336.

[5] *Letter to Trower*, 2 November 1818, 7:320.

[6] Ibid., 20 December 1818, 7:366, 368.

[7] *Speeches and Evidence*, 24 April 1823, 5:289.

resentation, would appear to establish a claim for Ricardian politics as being easily as advanced and democratic in principle as anything to be found in the writings of the other philosophical radicals.

James Mill's starting point in the consideration of the extent of the franchise, for example, bears all the hallmarks of utilitarianism. He set out to determine which individuals in the existing population possessed the capacity for political decision-making upon the premise that what was required for sound judgement and 'good' political choice was the full knowledge of one's own interest and the wherewithal to act rationally upon it. Mill then resolved the problem that individuals might be mistaken about their long-term interests in a straightforward manner. Education was the answer:

> The evils which arise from mistake are not incurable; for, if parties who act contrary to their interest had a proper knowledge of that interest, they would act well. What is necessary, then, is knowledge. Knowledge, on the part of those whose interests are the same as those of the community, would be an adequate remedy. But knowledge is a thing which is capable of being increased.[8]

At issue here, of course, is both what type of knowledge is necessary to politics and James Mill's conception of the relationship between improved knowledge and political order. On this subject, Mill adverts to the customary utilitarian conception of knowledge as individual mental capability, developed through education. On this line of reasoning, education is 'the means which may be employed to render the *mind*, as far as possible, an operative cause of happiness',[9] and improved education becomes instrumental to 'adopting the best means' to achieve that end.[10] The benefit of this to society is established courtesy of the familiar argument that if each individual secures the maximum amount of happiness possible, then the happiness of the nation (which is simply the aggregate of the happiness of the individuals who compose it) would also be at its maximum.

Not surprisingly, perhaps, this argument bears a strong family resemblance to that which John Stuart Mill would develop decades later. If individuals are seeking to act in ways which promote

[8] *Government*, p. 29.

[9] *Education*, p. 41; italics in original.

[10] Thus, in *Schools for All*, Mill writes of an aim 'to extirpate . . . ignorance by the force of education, and to plant knowledge in its stead' (p. 126).

their own interest (that is, in the pursuit of happiness/utility) they must possess full information not only of the alternatives available to them, but also of the utility they will derive once a particular course has been chosen. Now, this last requirement is the key to the problem of 'error'; for even if one knew the possibilities, one might not know the consequences (in terms of utility) of different actions. In their customary fashion, both of the Mills thus transformed the question of the extent of the franchise into a question about the extent of individual knowledge of consequences. If individuals had the knowledge, so runs the argument, they would not choose to elect 'demagogues and disturbers of the peace'—it would be contrary to their interests to do so.[11]

Ricardo, on the other hand, seems to have embarked upon a somewhat different course on his journey towards this same destination. He does not at all begin with the isolated utility maximizer, who needs 'knowledge' of the possibilities and consequences (in terms of 'happiness') of choice and action, in order efficiently to secure his goals. Nor is his an argument where the greatest good of society is discussed in concepts directly connected to the proposition that the best of all possible worlds will be the aggregate outcome of the efficient pursuit of individual utility maximization. For these reasons, Ricardo is not led to the question of judging the capacity for political decision-making on the part of the potential electorate in quite the same way as Mill. Though good government is, to be sure, that which secures the greatest good, the key to the novelty of Ricardo's argument is that he develops an alternative standard against which to measure the greatest good.[12]

The starting point of Ricardo's argument is quintessentially that of the classical economist. He begins with the familiar premise (dating back to François Quesnay and Adam Smith) that the material prosperity of the nation depends on 'the quantity of commodities annually produced'[13] or, what amounts to the same thing,

[11] This feature of the argument, allowed the Mills, by turns, to be educational reformers, supporters of the political emancipation of women, and advocates of plural voting.

[12] That Ricardo subscribed to this general view cannot be doubted, see *Letter to Mill*, 4 August 1822, 9:213.

[13] *Principles*, 1:277; see also p. 279.

the 'annual produce of the industry of the country'.[14] Good government, he claims, attends to material prosperity. Quite apart from the most obvious difference between this standard of well-being and that of 'general' utility (namely, that the former is directly quantifiable while the latter is not), the significance of focusing on material prosperity is that it leads Ricardo to formulate the question of the capacity of the electorate to decide in economic terms. Rather than insisting that individuals know their own interests, then, Ricardo is led to consider whether social groups know how material prosperity is best secured and whether they act in ways generally conducive to its growth.

Now, according to Ricardo, there are two ways of looking at annual production which need to be carefully distinguished in any discussion of material prosperity.[15] On the one hand, material well-being can be considered simply as the total quantity of commodities produced; on the other, it can be considered as the quantity of commodities produced after allowance had been made for that part of the total which would go to replace the commodities used to produce it (which, it is important to remember, for Ricardo included wage goods). Now, different judgements might be rendered as to the state of material prosperity according as one focused upon gross rather than net product. As Ricardo observed in a celebrated passage, Adam Smith 'constantly magnifies the advantages which a country derives from a large gross, rather than a large net income',[16] whereas the 'real interest of the nation' is rather more closely connected to net product and its disbursement.[17]

Many familiar Ricardian themes are contingent upon focusing on net product and its distribution between profits and rent. First, the claim that an increase in net product acts as a spur to economic growth follows from Ricardo's recognition that profits are the only source of revenue for accumulation—that is, for reproduction on an extended scale.[18] Since increased reproduction entails a greater

[14] *Letter to McCulloch*, 8:399.
[15] See *Principles*, 1:273–88.
[16] Ibid., p. 347.
[17] Ibid., p. 348.
[18] Thus, the celebrated argument that 'the wealth of a country may be increased in two ways: it may be increased by employing a greater proportion of revenue in the maintenance of productive labour . . . or it may be increased,

volume of employment for wage labourers, 'the labouring class have no small interest in the manner in which the net income of the country is expended'.[19] Furthermore, the idea that the use of these surpluses for the purchase of luxuries acts as a drag on the rate of growth rests on this proposition, so that workers 'must naturally desire that as much of the revenue as possible should be diverted from expenditure on luxuries'.[20] The proposition that 'there are no taxes which have not a tendency to lessen the power to accumulate'[21] is one of its corollaries, since 'the power of paying taxes is in proportion to net, and not in proportion to gross' product.[22] Lastly, perhaps the most celebrated of all Ricardian doctrines, the idea that restrictions on the free trade in corn are detrimental to the national interest also rests upon it. That story is simple enough. A rise in the price of corn consequent upon restrictions on its importation, has the effect of driving cultivation onto less fertile lands and so of raising the rents received by landlords at the expense of the profits of the farmer. The ultimate effect of the fall in profits is a reduction in the power to accumulate.

Some less well known Ricardian themes, however, are contingent upon focusing on gross product. In particular, the idea of wealth, or riches as Ricardo customarily refers to it, is in certain contexts better understood by considering gross rather than net product. Riches, argues Ricardo, depend upon the 'abundance' of

---

without employing any additional quantity of labour, by making the same quantity more productive' (*Principles* 1:278). It is perhaps worth observing that when Marx decided to substitute the term 'surplus value' for 'net product', the accumulation process described here by Ricardo was given a whole new social significance; for it enabled Marx to describe it as the process of extracting (absolute and relative) surplus value.

[19] *Principles*, 1:392.

[20] Ibid., p. 393. The point that had to be understood, according to Ricardo, was that while 'all the productions of a country are consumed . . . it makes the greatest difference imaginable whether they are consumed by those who reproduce, or by those who do not reproduce another value. When we say that revenue is saved, and added to capital, what we mean is, that the portion of revenue, so said to be added to capital, is consumed by productive instead of unproductive labourers' (*Principles* 1:151n*).

[21] *Principles*, 1:152. Interestingly, as Ricardo reminded McCulloch in 1820, '[I]t is only because taxation interferes with the accumulation of capital, and diminishes the demand for labour, that it is injurious to the working classes' (*Letter to McCulloch*, 29 March 1820, 8:168–69).

[22] *Principles* 1:349. See also *Notes on Malthus*, 2:381–82.

commodities produced,[23] so that if one is, say, comparing the wealth of the nation at two different points in time, or comparing the wealth of two different countries, then it is to the gross product that he recommends us to turn. This is why, as we shall see shortly, Ricardo became skeptical as to the universally beneficial effects of the introduction of machinery on the economic state of the nation which, though always accompanied by an increase in net product, may be associated with a decrease in gross product. It also explains why improvements in the division of labour (increases in the productivity of a given labour force) were for Ricardo the generally preferred mode of increasing riches.[24]

The whole thing can be put rather more succinctly. When the task is to understand the potential for future growth (that is, to judge the prospects for economic progress), Ricardo invariably consults net product. When the task is concerned instead with assessing the existing state of the nation, Ricardo consults gross product.

With these essentials of Ricardian economics in mind, it is a relatively straightforward matter to see the originality in his mode of addressing the suffrage question: Ricardo made the question of the extent of the franchise turn on the relationship between democratic participation and material well-being in one or other of these dimensions (albeit in a quite complex way). It need hardly be said that the link Ricardo thereby established between the suffrage question and material prosperity entails a relationship between his economics and his politics of a rather more compelling nature than just that it aids in 'directing government to right measures' (though it will certainly be useful in that arena as well).[25] Economic science became in Ricardo's hands the stablemate to the 'science of politics' itself.

The idea that the general question of political organization could be analysed from an economic point of view was stated quite explicitly by Ricardo in the first of his two discourses on politics, *Observations on Parliamentary Reform*:

[23] Ibid., p. 275.

[24] Ibid., p. 279.

[25] Not to put too fine a point on it, Paul Samuelson's claim that the classical economists 'lived during the industrial revolution, but scarcely looked out from their libraries to notice the remaking of the world' is, quite frankly, ridiculous ('The canonical classical model', p. 1428).

Although it may be true that the country has flourished with a House of Commons constituted as ours has been, it must be shown that such a constitution of it is favourable to the prosperity of the country.[26]

In setting himself the task of producing an argument for a democratic polity on the grounds that it tended to promote material prosperity, Ricardo stands in contrast to James Mill, who, as we have seen, made the extent of the franchise turn on the relationship between his more directly individualistic premises of democratic participation and rising individual 'mental qualities' or improved 'levels' of personal development.[27] This contrast is brought into sharp relief when one looks at how Ricardo went about making the case that workers had the capacity for political decision-making. For here, Ricardo's argument not only challenged the basis of virtual representation (even in the attenuated form that it was retained by the Mills), but it also brings forward the value of public opinion in a manner different from James Mill.[28]

There are a number of quite striking examples of this, but perhaps one of the clearest is closely bound up with Ricardo's most famous theoretical *volte face*—the revision of his opinion on the subject of the effects of the introduction of machinery.[29] Indeed, the fact that the value of the common opinion of workers was confirmed by the observation that workers correctly comprehended the effects of the introduction of machinery was not lost on Ricardo.[30] He went out of his way to say so in the new chapter on machinery in the third edition of the *Principles* (1821):

[26] *Works and Correspondence*, 5:499.

[27] Having noted this, it will be apparent that one could utilize it to unearth a distinction between James Mill and John Stuart Mill on the one hand, and between James Mill and Ricardo on the other. James Mill's essay on *Government* contains both approaches to securing the greatest good. At one point he speaks (reminiscent of Ricardo) of 'greatest possible quantity of the produce of his labour' (*Government*, p. 5), while at another he speaks of interest as 'preference' in a manner more like his son.

[28] This would seem to fit well with Coats's observation that Mill had a 'tendency to give priority to moral . . . considerations, over merely economic ones' (*The Classical Economists and Economic Policy*, p. 13).

[29] The story of this change of opinion is well known. The reader may consult the editorial introduction to Ricardo's *Works and Correspondence* (1:lvii–lx) for further details.

[30] Nor was it lost on Malthus who wrote: 'You have used one expression which

The opinion entertained by the labouring class, that the employment of machinery is frequently detrimental to their interests, is not
founded on prejudice or error, but is conformable to the correct
principles of political economy.[31]

Ricardo's reasoning on the subject is simple enough; 'as plain as
any proposition in geometry' as he told McCulloch. When the introduction of machinery (which is *always* associated with an increase in net product) is accompanied by a decrease in gross product it will be 'very injurious to the interests of the class of
labourers'[32] and, what is more, it will diminish 'the means of en-
joyment of some one, or more, classes of the community'.[33] He re-
iterated the claim on the floor of the House of Commons in May
1823, declaring that machinery 'must, in some degree, operate
prejudicially to the working classes'.[34]

But while the reasoning is straightforward, its interpretation has
turned out to be rather more problematic. The interpretive question is this: to what context does the argument apply?

Received opinion seems to hold that it refers essentially to the
immediate, or temporary effects of the introduction of machinery,
and that the difficulty is, therefore, likely to be short lived. This
was certainly the construction John Stuart Mill put on it nearly
thirty years later:

All increase of fixed capital [machinery], when it takes place at the
expense of circulating, must be, *at least temporarily*, prejudicial to
the interests of the labourers. . . . Nevertheless, I do not believe
that as things are actually transacted, improvements in production

---

is liable to be taken fast hold of by the labouring class' (*Letter to Ricardo*, 16 July
1821, 9:18). McCulloch also saw the political implications, and seems to have
become almost apoplectic when he read the offending chapter: 'If your reasoning
. . . be well founded, the laws against the Luddites are a disgrace to the Statute
book. Let me beg you to reconsider this subject' (*Letter to Ricardo*, 5 June 1821,
8:385).

[31] *Principles*, 1:392. In contrast, as late as 1846 Henry Brougham was still trying
to attribute 'the rage against machinery' to 'ignorance of economical science'
(quoted in Crane Brinton's *English Political Thought*, pp. 33–34). Ricardo's statement seems to make it very clear just who he thought was ignorant of the economical science, and who (therefore) was prejudiced in this matter.

[32] *Principles* 1:388.

[33] *Letter to McCulloch*, 18 June 1821, 8:388.

[34] *Speeches and Evidence*, 30 May 1823, 5:303.

are often, if ever, injurious, even temporarily, to the labouring classes in the aggregate.[35]

This construal of Ricardo's meaning is given increased credibility by some remarks he makes at the end of the same chapter to the effect that 'the statements that I have made will not, I hope, lead to the inference that machinery should not be encouraged'.[36] The basic idea, then, is that any deleterious effects attributed to the introduction of machinery by Ricardo should be taken to refer exclusively to short-run disequilibria and to the problems involved in making a transition from the old to the new equilibrium.

It will be immediately apparent that if this reading is accurate, then Ricardo's argument would hardly be supportive of the need to place value on the common opinion of the labouring classes, for in this instance it would confirm rather that the opinion was very shortsighted. Indeed, were this to be the case, the proposition would furnish the basis for an argument (just like John Stuart Mill's) which demonstrated that *no* weight should be attached to the opinion. A longer view would be what was called for.

But there are good grounds for taking up an alternative reading. In the first place, John Stuart Mill's interpretation, as just outlined, seems to reduce to an argument about the effects of machinery essentially equivalent to the one Ricardo had actually held *before* he declared himself to have changed his mind. This earlier argument was set out by Ricardo in his speech to the House of Commons in December 1819 in the debate over a motion to establish a select committee to inquire into certain 'plans' of Robert Owen; a debate in which the question of the effects of machinery had come up. Ricardo then had held that while 'it could not be denied that, on the whole view of the subject, . . . machinery did not lessen the demand for labour',[37] it might be 'mis-applied' in a particular industry. This, Ricardo recognised, might occasion an overproduction in that *particular* industry (together with a *temporary* dislocation of workers in the industry), but it could neither be general nor lasting. Indeed, the *British Press* reported this part of Ricardo's intervention as follows:

[35] *Political Economy*, I.vi, §2 & §3; italics added.
[36] *Principles*, 1:395.
[37] *Speeches and Evidence*, 16 December 1819, 5:31.

[Mr. Ricardo] never could think that machinery could do mischief to any country, either in its immediate or its permanent effect. Machinery, indeed, in one way might be carried too far, that is where it is employed in the manufacture of a particular commodity, as for instance, in the manufacture of cotton, but where the individual extended it too far it would not repay him, and he would be soon obliged to reduce it, or employ it in another channel.[38]

This kind of argument, if we are to believe John Stuart Mill, is also to be found in the new chapter on machinery. Unfortunately for Mill, however, when it is recalled that this later argument (of 1821) was heralded by Ricardo as a great 'change of mind'—and this quite explicitly (both in the third edition of the *Principles* and on the floor of the House of Commons)—it is difficult to place much faith in a rendition of this new and changed argument that would have us believe that it turns out to be exactly the *same* argument Ricardo had maintained before his *change* of mind.

This, however, is not the only idiosyncracy about the received opinion. Theoretically speaking, a tolerably convincing case can be made out to the effect that the new argument is actually an exercise in comparative statics rather than an analysis of temporary effects consequent upon the need to make the transition to a new equilibrium. For not only are exercises in comparative statics the staple of Ricardo's technique of theorising (as he was wont to put it, they allowed him to emphasise the permanent effects of changes[39]), but it is very clear that they are exactly what Ricardo engages in his famous numerical example in the machinery chapter. If it is an exercise in comparative statics, then the opinion that the demand for labour may fall consequent upon the introduction of machinery, is not shortsighted.

The above should not be taken to imply that before his change of mind on the subject of machinery, Ricardo had given any less weight to the opinions of the labouring classes on the matter. In fact, the reverse seems to be true; but he had done so on different grounds. As is well known, Ricardo had voted against the Six Acts

---

[38] *Works and Correspondence*, 5:31n.1. Just what led Ricardo to change his mind on this point need not detain us here. It is worth observing, however, that one commentator put it down to the influence of 'the propaganda of Owen and the Owenites' (Max Beer, *History of British Socialism* 1:149).

[39] *Letter to Malthus*, 24 January 1817, 7:120.

which were promulgated after the massacre at Peterloo; and in speaking against one of them (the Seditious Meetings Prevention Bill) on the floor of the House of Commons on 6 December 1819 he made it perfectly clear that he was not for prohibiting such opinions, but rather for having them better represented in that very House.[40] What is more, he had made a very similar argument in correspondence to Trower two months before which renders visible the basis of this earlier argument:

> One word on the Manchester proceedings. . . . I hope that no law can be produced to justify the violent interference of magistrates to dissolve a meeting of the people, the avowed object of which was to petition legally for a redress of real or imagined grievances. If the right to petition is only to be exercised at the discretion of magistrates, or of any other body in the state, then it is a farce to call us a free people. These large assemblages of the people are to be regretted—they may in their consequences be productive of mischief, but if the security of our freedom depends on our right to assemble and state our wrongs, which in the absence of real representation I believe it does, then we must patiently suffer the lesser evil to avoid the greater.[41]

Here the argument seems to rest on a direct correspondence between genuine representation and the actualization of political freedom. Ricardo's reference to the grievances as being 'real or imagined', as if the verdict might go either way, is indicative of the weight he was placing here on a purely political argument. The point was that it did not matter whether the complaints were real or imagined—inadequate representation precluded the opinions from being registered as they should be registered if freedom was to be secured as justice mandated. Once Ricardo had availed himself of his new-found theoretical principle on the effects of machinery, which confirmed the grievance to be real and not imagined,

---

[40] *Speeches and Evidence*, 6 December 1819, 5:28–29. When Ricardo had spoken in the new chapter on machinery of not being aware of needing to retract anything he had published on the subject, he may not have had clearly in his mind the following passage from the *Essay on Profits*: 'The effects on the interest of [the labouring] class, would be nearly the same as the effects of improved machinery, which it is now no longer questioned, has a decided tendency to raise the real wages of labour' (4:35).

[41] *Letter to Trower*, 25 September 1819, 8:80.

the result was only to strengthen the basis of his support for the representation of common opinion by giving it an additional grounding in his economics in a manner it had not enjoyed before.

Ricardo deferred to the common opinion of workers as being in conformity with the 'correct principles of the political economy' and so, as he argued, with the interest of the community as a whole, in numerous other instances. 'The working class', he once wrote to Francis Place, 'are often cruelly calumniated'.[42] Another striking example of his confidence in the opinion of workers came in his opposition to a proposed act (in 1823) to increase by statute the number of apprentices taken on board all vessels of the Merchant Marine. Ricardo spoke against this measure in the House of Commons on three separate occasions (13 & 24 March, and 18 April 1823),[43] each time making the point that the proposed act was drafted exclusively in the interests of employers; and that they sought only to lower wages. He urged the Honourable Members opposite to consult the seamen, who would be able to acquaint them with the real motive and the true effect. None of this sounds like the voice of the friend of the bourgeoisie.[44] Furthermore, the relative frequency with which Ricardo cites instances like these, where workers came to form the correct opinion (that is, an opinion conformable to the interest of the nation), suggests that they were not necessarily a special or limited class of cases.[45]

[42] *Letter to Place*, 9 September 1821, 9:54.

[43] *Speeches and Evidence*, 5:273, 276–77.

[44] There is a striking passage in a letter to James Brown, written during the stagnation of 1819, which seems at once to re-inforce the very opposite opinion (namely that Ricardo was very much concerned over the condition of the working class) and to place in a clearer light his alleged tendency to focus exclusively on long-run rather than short-run effects. The remark, it should be noted, is made in the context of a discussion of the effects of introducing one of Ricardo's favourite policies; a freer trade in corn: 'We all have to lament the present distressed state of the labouring classes in this country, but the remedy is not very apparent to me. The correcting of our errors of legislation with regard to trade would *ultimately* be of considerable service to all classes of the community, but it would afford no immediate relief . . . the derangement which such measures would occasion in the actual employment of capital, and the changes which would become necessary, would rather aggravate than relieve the distress under which we are now labouring' (*Letter to Brown*, 13 October 1819, 8:103; italics added).

[45] Thus, in *Parliamentary Reform*, Ricardo spoke of an unjustified 'presumption of mistaken views of interest' entertained by the ruling classes with respect to their inferiors (5:502).

The one notable exception to this rule seems to have been Ricardo's position on the old Poor Laws, to which he was fervently opposed.[46] The paradox, of course, is not so much that this opposition diminishes his credentials as being a 'friend to the poor'.[47] It would be difficult to prosecute that case, given that Ricardo was the first to admit the misery labourers experienced in times of depression, and that he insisted that any project for the removal of existing legislation had to be slow and gradual. Rather, the paradox is that Ricardo spoke with such a conviction of the need to 'teach the labouring classes that they must themselves provide for those casualties to which they are exposed',[48] that one is led to wonder why it was that the poor themselves did not learn that the Poor Laws ran directly counter to the principles of political economy (at least, that is, in the version they were expounded by Ricardo), and so to their own (and the nation's) interests.

Ricardo does, however, provide us with a clue as to the resolution of this paradox. As it turns out, it is a clue which might be just as helpful in explaining the rule as it is in explaining the exception. According to Ricardo, the failure of the poor to comprehend the 'pernicious tendency of these laws' was the direct consequence of their having lived for too long within a culture, itself the immediate product of those laws, where social norms and values were such as to render it impossible for them even to begin to do so. The Poor Laws had 'been so long established', argued Ricardo, that 'the habits of the poor' had been 'formed upon their operation'.[49] This idea, that character and culture were closely related in this way, differed hardly at all from that of a much more famous

[46] One other case where Ricardo berated the opinions of workers, namely the Spitalfields silk weavers (whose employment contract was underwritten by special legislation), does not seem to stand as a glaring exception to the rule. Ricardo's argument here was that the Spitalfields weavers enjoyed their local privileges at the expense of weavers in other parts of the country. That is, what Ricardo opposed was the idea that the interests of a faction of a class should be allowed to dominate the interests of the class as a whole.

[47] *Principles*, 1:106 (the phrase is repeated on p. 107).

[48] *Letter to Trower*, 26 January 1818, 7:248. The parallel passage in the *Principles* runs as follows: 'By impressing on the poor the value of independence, by teaching them that they must look not to systematic or casual charity, but to their own exertions for support, . . . we shall by degrees approach a sounder and more healthful state' (1:107).

[49] *Principles*, 1:106.

friend of the poor, Robert Owen. In his *New View of Society*, Owen had argued that 'the direct and certain effects' of the Poor Laws were to 'injure the poor', because 'they prepare the poor to acquire the worst habits, and practice every kind of crime'.[50] Nevertheless, it must be said that on the general question of the poor, Ricardo did not advance far beyond the opinions of other reformers. Here the influence of Malthus's principle of population seems to have been the decisive factor in shaping his views. So wedded was he to this, that he proposed no policies which might alleviate the sufferings of the poor if, on that principle, they would contribute to further population increase.[51]

If the exclusion of the poor from normal economic life was deployed in this manner by Ricardo to sustain his well-known position on their general incapacity for citizenship in the prevailing economic circumstances, it seems natural enough to look to the inclusion of others (especially workers) in economic life to illuminate his more general point about the extensiveness of the reasonable part of the country. Since workers certainly did not acquire it from books, or from schools, the only possible forum left where they might have developed their capacities was in the school of life. While Ricardo would not have differed with Jane Marcet, author of the popular *Conversations on Political Economy*, over her idea that 'a more general knowledge of political economy' would be productive of 'no trifling good',[52] and while he even applauded her own efforts to make the science more widely available, it is perfectly clear that his confidence in the reasonable people was not premised on their first having undertaken a formal course of instruction in the science.

At this juncture, it is instructive to return for a moment to the contrast between Ricardo's arguments for the enfranchisement of

[50] *New View of Society*, pp. 141–42.

[51] Thus, while Ricardo actually funded the establishment of a school on Lancasterian principles for both boys and girls in Minchinhampton in 1816, he declined a request to contribute the sum of £50 to a scheme Brougham had launched for the schooling of the poor in London if the daily programme entailed feeding the children. More modern moral sentiments with regard to the treatment of the poor recoil at this—others of Ricardo's time did not. James Mill hastily wrote back to Ricardo, urging him to fund the London project, since Brougham had never intended actually to feed the children. (See *Letter to Mill*, 12 December 1818, 7:360 and subsequent correspondence.)

[52] *Conversations*, p. 11.

the working class and those of James Mill with which this chapter opened. In the essay on *Government*, Mill had also considered the question of how far one might extend the franchise in the face of existing instances of popular protest and unrest amongst the labouring classes. He, too, considered the value of the common opinions of the labouring classes as they were expressed in the self-same gatherings that Ricardo had defended in Parliament (before Mill's essay appeared) and had none too eliptically alluded to them in the chapter on machinery. Here is what James Mill had to say:

> What signify the irregularities of the mob, more than half composed in the greater number of instances, of boys and women, and disturbing for a few hours or days a particular town? What signifies the occasional turbulence of a manufacturing district, peculiarly unhappy from a very great deficiency of a middle rank, as there the population almost wholly consists of rich manufacturers and poor workmen; with whose minds no pains are taken by anybody; with whose afflictions there is no virtuous family of the middle rank to sympathize; whose children have no good example of such a family to see and to admire; and who are placed in the highly unfavourable situation of fluctuating between very high wages in one year, and very low wages in another? It is altogether futile with regard to the foundation of good government to say that this or the other portion of the people, may at this, or the other time, depart from the wisdom of the middle rank.[53]

While this should not be taken to indicate that Mill wished to deny democratic citizenship to the working class,[54] it does indicate that Mill's argument for enfranchising them differs from anything deployed by Ricardo. There is nothing in Ricardo, for example, about needing to educate men and women to correct opinions, or about having them emulate those 'virtuous families of the middle rank' that Mill advocates. Ricardo simply held that these individuals were to be represented as a matter of principle. For Mill, it

[53] *Government*, p. 32.

[54] Although, since Mill does remark that better than half of the mob were 'women and boys', they would all be disqualified on the grounds of age and gender by Mill in any case—despite their riotous assembly. Indeed, was not 'males over the age of forty' James Mill's electorate (*Government*, p. 22)? If so, most of the mob would not be voting anyway.

was essential to the argument to show that most of the time, most of the people 'continue to be guided by that rank'.[55] Nothing of this kind seems to have been present in Ricardo's argument.

There is, however, another feature of Mill's reasoning on this subject that should not be allowed to pass without comment, since it further highlights the contrast with Ricardo. Mill claimed that these instances of popular unrest should, in fact, be regarded as an 'exception' to the rule that the people were capable of judging. Already, one might note, his reasoning is contrary to that of Ricardo, for whom these protests represented the perfectly normal expression of a 'correct' and not 'mistaken' opinion. Like a good lawyer not satisfied with the brilliance of his performance, Mill next proceeds to argue that these exceptions actually *prove* the rule.[56] Since there are so few of these protesters (measured against the whole population), clearly most are guided by those middling ranks of people of good sense. Interestingly enough, for Ricardo, not only was such guidance unnecessary, but it might turn out to be counter-productive. As we have already seen, Ricardo was very well aware that individuals belonged to particular social classes and that class interests diverged; what he wanted from democracy was the representation of these interests, not the elimination of all of them save those of the middle class.

This confidence in the capacity of members of the working class to come to correct conclusions on matters concerning the well-being of the nation pervades Ricardo's politics; and it is uniformly legitimated by an appeal to the 'science of political economy'. In no small measure, this helps to explain why Ricardo's proposals as to the extent of the suffrage stand much closer to those originally expounded by Bentham (universality) than to those proposed by either James Mill or, in his later writings, John Stuart Mill.

And what applied to workers, applied also to disenfranchised

[55] *Government*, p. 32. There would seem, therefore, to be more than a grain of truth in the judgement passed (in the context of another of Mill's essays) by one historian on James Mill's 'democratic' thought: '[Mill] was championing certain "outs" who wished to get in. He was no defender of liberty or equality in the abstract. The lower class, "brutalized", undiscriminating, the prey of violent demagogues, in his opinion obviously could no more be trusted than the aristocracy. Clearly the article [on the *Edinburgh Review* in 1824] was never written by a thorough-going democrat' (Nesbitt, *Benthamite Reviewing*, p. 42).

[56] *Government*, p. 32, et seq.

small manufacturers; and for the same reason—they, too, were capable of forming political opinions conformable to interests of the nation:

> The reasoning by which the liberty of trade is supported, is so powerful, that it is daily obtaining converts. It is with pleasure, that I see the progress which this great principle is making amongst those whom we should have expected to cling the longest to old prejudices.[57]

In this pamphlet Ricardo goes on to provide a concrete example of a group of Gloucestershire clothiers who petitioned Parliament in 1816 for the removal of the corn laws. The petition offered a *quid pro quo*, suggesting that the dismantling of the protection of agriculture could be accompanied by the removal of the protection enjoyed by their own industry, that Ricardo warmly commended. It is of the first importance to notice that on Ricardo's argument, these sections of the population were to be represented not because they numbered among those good and virtuous people of the middle rank (as James Mill might have put it). Instead, their claim to representation as formulated by Ricardo was no different than that of workers; a capacity for judgement congruent with both their own and the community's interest in economic prosperity.

But in Ricardo's hands, the sword of participatory democracy was double-edged. Not only did Ricardo wield it so as to construct a positive case for thorough-going parliamentary reform, he used it, too, to construct a negative case against existing constitutional arrangements. The basic claim, of course, was the standard fare of philosophical radicalism: participatory democracy was the nation's only security against the domination of politics by sinister interests. However, in developing it, Ricardo once again mobilized the science of political economy to political ends in a manner not attempted by the other philosophical radicals of the day.

Exemplary of this particular use of an economic argument for democratic participation is Ricardo's sustained assault on the conduct of monetary policy by successive Tory governments. Commencing with the Bullion Controversy of 1809–1810, Ricardo had consistently maintained that bankers and, more especially, the directors of the Bank of England, had been pursuing their own in-

[57] *Economical and Secure Currency*, 1816, 4:70.

terests in direct opposition to, and at the expense of, the national interest.[58] According to Ricardo, the actual space for the exercise of these sinister interests had been opened up by a complex combination of circumstances; the precondition for which had been Parliament's act to suspend specie payments in 1797. By removing this legislative restriction on the Bank of England's ability to issue paper currency, but while still allowing it to enjoy a monopoly of note issue, this act had set in motion a sort of self-reinforcing vicious cycle. Remembering that it was always open to the Bank's directors to augment their profits by issuing paper currency (in the form of loans at interest or the discounting of bills) in excess of the underlying monetary base (gold stocks), and remembering too that these overissues, as they were called, were (according to standard quantity theory conclusions) inflationary, a situation had arisen whereby the interest of the community (price stability) was opposed to the interests of the monetary authorities (bank profits); and the problem was that the monetary authorities had the power to act on their interests, while the community was powerless to stop them.

Given Ricardo's self-confessed delight at attacking the Bank of England ('I always enjoy any attack upon the Bank',[59] he once confided to Malthus), it is not surprising that he entered the fray with vigour. Against the abovementioned (and other) illiberal practices, Ricardo mustered a number of arguments.

In the first place, he mounted a moral crusade (one that had been suggested to him by James Mill) against the Bank being allowed to appropriate to itself the profits derived from the use of deposits of public funds. The public, on Ricardo's thinking, were in 'justice' entitled to remuneration, while the Bank was in 'gratitude' bound 'voluntarily to relinquish to the state, the whole benefit'[60] derived from these deposits. Ricardo calculated that

---

[58] There is a parallel between this argument and his opposition to oligarchy and his rejection of a politics of virtue that we discussed in chapter 2—not unlike those virtual representatives, the Bank directors might follow their own sinister interest to the detriment of the nation.

[59] *Letter to Malthus*, 10 September 1815, 6:268–69.

[60] *Economical and Secure Currency*, 4:93. Writing to Malthus in the period leading up to the publication of this pamphlet, Ricardo stated: 'I think the Bank an unnecessary establishment getting rich by those profits which *fairly* belong to the public' (*Letter to Malthus*, 10 September 1815, 6:268; italics added).

from this source the Bank had secured to its own benefit (between 1806 and 1816) some £3.8m in profits; and this, directly at the expense of the public. He was especially outraged that the Bank (that is, the owners of Bank stock) was actually claiming a *right* to these purloined profits under their Charter:

> Is it not lamentable to view a great and opulent body like the Bank of England, exhibiting a wish to augment their hoards by undue gains wrested from the hands of an overburthened people?[61]

Ricardo repeated essentially the same argument in Parliament years later; although he does appear to have toned it down a little by attributing the conduct of the directors of the Bank rather more to their 'error' of 'not knowing how to manage [their own concerns] upon true principles',[62] than to moral turpitude. *Hansard* reported him as follows:

> With regard to the directors, he was willing, at all times, to give them full credit for honesty of intention; but he could not help thinking, that they had at different times involved the country in considerable difficulties.[63]

Unfortunately, moral condemnation took Ricardo only so far. The directors' retort was that they were legitimately judged in their conduct by the proprietors of Bank stock at regular intervals (elections took place annually), and that this method of judgement was to be preferred to 'all the theories of modern philosophers on the subject'.[64] That a director should have preferred this mode of as-

---

[61] *Economical and Secure Currency*, 4:93. This particular argument was suggested to him by James Mill. Indeed, Ricardo seems to have copied it word for word from Mill's letter into the text of his pamphlet. Mill had written '[h]old up to view unsparingly the infamy of a great and opulent body like the bank, exhibiting a wish to augment its hoards by undue gains wrested from the hands of an overburthened people' (*Letter from Mill*, 3 January 1816, 7:5). Ricardo was not alone in this crusade and, as Fetter noted in his *British Monetary Orthodoxy*, '[M]en who were far apart on most points were in agreement that someone was making too much money from the paper money system' (p. 70).

[62] *Speeches and Evidence*, 8 March 1822, 5:143. He added that 'the directors had convinced him by their conduct that they did not know what they were about' (p. 144).

[63] *Speeches and Evidence*, 8 March 1822, 5:143.

[64] These are the words of one Mr. Pearse, himself a Bank director. They are reported by Sraffa in the editorial apparatus attached to Ricardo's speech (*Works and Correspondence*, 5:143).

sessment is not at all surprising; one would hardly expect those to whom Bank profits were being distributed as dividends, to vote out the current directors in favour of others whose actions might better conform to Ricardo's code of conduct; it would be against their own interests to do so. Furthermore, this was not the only argument forwarded by the Bank against its critics. It was also maintained that the Bank's policy, far from being detrimental to the national interest, was actually beneficial to it. This claim rested upon the articulation of a relation between economic activity, credit creation, the supply of money, and the price level that differed from the one offered by Ricardo. Grounded on the real-bills doctrine, the Bank's case was that its own activities had been dictated entirely by the needs of trade, so that its issue of paper money was not (and, according to some of its more extreme proponents, could not be) in excess. Since this argument was to gain influential political support at the time (in the person of Nicholas Vansittart at the Exchequer), and important theoretical support some twenty years later in the debate surrounding the Bank Act of 1844 (in the persons of Thomas Tooke and John Fullarton[65]), it is clear that the moral condemnation of the Bank of England had its limitations.

Ricardo's second line of attack saw him deploy an argument bringing forward the value of free information as a check to what he saw as existing abuses of the Bank:

> But the public attention has been lately called to the affairs of the Bank; and the subject of their profits is generally canvassed and understood.[66]

While both of these challenges were not without their own force, it is well to note that they had both been suggested to Ricardo by

[65] This is not the place to explore the theoretical issues at stake in these debates; except to say that everything hinged on the domain of applicability of the quantity theory of money and, specifically, whether its conclusions could be applied to the short run as readily as they could be applied to the long run (on this point see Green, 'Money, output and inflation in classical economics'). The quite different assessment of the Bank of England's policy that the anti-Ricardian theory mandated was nicely summarized by Tooke: 'The Bank, on the contrary, was enabled, by the Restriction Act, to relieve the distress. . . . The Directors extended their discounts very considerably in 1810; and . . . they thus only filled the vacuum in the circulation' (*History of Prices*, p. 123).

[66] *Economical and Secure Currency*, 4:114.

James Mill. Ricardo's third avenue of attack, however, appears to have been utterly original to him. In it he maintained that a public check, not just a change of economic policy, or a sacking of the Bank's current directors, or even threats to remove its existing Charter, was the ultimate channel through which such abuses could be controlled permanently. *Hansard* reported the speech in which Ricardo made this argument as follows:

> [Mr. Ricardo] did not think this a question only between the Bank and ministers . . . , but rather between ministers and the Bank on the one side, and the country on the other.[67]

With this argument, of course, Ricardo immediately distanced himself from both the Whigs and the Tory liberals (like William Huskisson); and this, despite the fact that all three of these groups favoured roughly the same change of policy (control over excessive note issue). Unlike Ricardo, the two existing parties (and here one should also include the majority of Tories who had sided with Nicholas Vansittart against the Bullion Report in 1811) seem to have viewed the underlying issue as exclusively one about the appropriate design of monetary policy. Whatever their position on that score, then, they uniformly saw the question entirely as a matter 'between ministers and the Bank'. For Whigs, who regularly criticised the Tory Government's lax financial policies, a sufficient solution was that Tory ministers be replaced by Whig ministers. For the Tory liberals, the solution was the resumption of specie payments; a measure they succeeded in carrying in 1819. But Ricardo had introduced an entirely novel idea concerning the ultimate check on the conduct of monetary policy—for that check was to be exercised by the country itself (or, more accurately, 'the reasonable part' of it), and not just by the theories of the political economists as imbibed by the legislators. The idea of this kind of direct public involvement in politics was (and is) remarkable. It contrasts sharply with both the traditional Benthamite confidence in professional expertise in government, and the more modern theories of democracy which give similar primacy to elites in policy-making and relegates the people to simply choosing among elites.[68] This, of course, is not to say that Ricardo depreciated the

[67] *Speeches and Evidence*, 24 May 1819, 5:9–10.
[68] There is an interesting discussion of just where John Stuart Mill's subsequent

value of expert advice in the formulation of government policy. His own contributions in that regard are sufficient to dispel that inference. What appears rather to have been the case is that the requisite knowledge for useful inputs into politics was not seen by Ricardo to have been the exclusive preserve of experts. This is what is distinctive about his argument over the conduct of monetary policy.

It is impossible to leave this subject without reminding ourselves that certain modern quantity theorists seem to have taken an altogether different route to the solution of the conduct of monetary policy. Some of their number have preferred to advocate drawing up and enacting a strict set of rules—sometimes legislative rules of self-command (like balanced-budget amendments), sometimes quantitative controls on bank reserves (like monetary base controls), sometimes both—on the presumption that these fixed rules will act to direct the conduct of monetary policy into 'scientifically correct' channels. To be sure, still others of their number have taken the free banking route, of having no monetary regulation at all, not even of note issue; no central bank, no lender of last resort. Yet the impulse behind these strategies turns out to be essentially the same; the idea is to remove from the hands of politicians all 'technical' decisions concerning the regulation of the currency.

What is noteworthy about both of these contemporary approaches is the fact that they go directly against the course of action advocated by Ricardo. While his approach was to seek to place the conduct of monetary policy squarely within the political arena, contemporary quantity theorists seem to want to do just the opposite. In either of its contemporary manifestations, the campaign is for the complete removal of the formulation of monetary policy from the sphere of political discourse. It is tempting to speculate as to whether such attempts may be due, in part, to the fact that (unlike Ricardo) these modern exponents of the quantity theory do not have near the confidence that public opinion will uniformly be led to see the desirability ('scientific correctness') of quantity theory recommendations. But in that event, all that we should have discovered is nothing more than that their democratic commit-

contributions to politics might fit in this context in Dennis Thompson's *John Stuart Mill and Representative Government*, p. 21.

ment comes to its limit when faced with the prospect of their favourite theories being exploded in the domain of public opinion. Quite how Ricardo himself might have faced up to that worrying possibility, we shall return to consider after we have completed our outline of all of the strands that go to make up his political thought.[69]

However, unless it be thought that Ricardo's argument against the Bank of England was merely an isolated instance of the idea that effective economic decision-making at the level of government was not only a matter of getting the policy right, but that it was also intimately bound up with the democratic or undemocratic constitution of political society itself, it is worth remarking that it is a theme which appears again and again throughout his thinking about politics. Another example of its influence is to be found in Ricardo's famous campaign against government loan expenditure and, in particular, against the burden of a national debt which, by 1820, was in excess of £800m.[70] His 'wild sort of notion', as Mallet called it,[71] involved a proposal to pay off the whole of the national debt by means of a one-time tax on property, a capital levy, so that 'by one great effort, we should get rid of one of the most terrible scourges which was ever invented to afflict a nation'.[72] When he set out the details of the plan in 1820, Ricardo's idea seems to have been that the debt would be retired over two or three years. By 1823 he was advocating that it be retired over 'two, three, six or twelve months'.[73] It goes without saying that Ricardo's plan did not

[69] That is, in chapter 7 below.

[70] See Hargreaves, *The National Debt*, Table B, p. 292; Mitchell, *British Historical Statistics*, Table XI.7, p. 601; Cook and Stevenson, *British Historical Facts*, p. 187.

[71] See the editorial annotations in *Works and Correspondence*, 8:147n.1.

[72] *Funding System* 4:197. Ricardo had given the idea an airing in 1817 in the *Principles* (1:248), and he floated it again in the House of Commons in 1819 (*Speeches and Evidence*, 24 December 1819, 5:38) before it appeared in the Supplement to the *Encyclopedia Britannica* in 1820. The fact that Ricardo's proposed tax was not to be levied on those 'whose incomes are derived from wages or salaries' (*Letter to McCulloch*, 15 September 1820, 8:238) caused some critical comment at the time, and warrants mention here only insofar as it speaks to the caricature of Ricardo as the class enemy of the wage-earner.

[73] *Speeches and Evidence*, 11 March 1823, 5:271. The poet Percy Bysshe Shelley, interestingly enough, had the same thought in 1820 (see his unpublished *Philosophical View of Reform*, pp. 34–37).

receive a particularly auspicious reception in the circles that counted:

> [A]s it usually happens I am attacked by the most opposite parties. By some stockholders I am accused of not doing justice to them, by suggesting that they are not fairly entitled, in ready money, to £100, for £100–3pc^{ts}, but to the market price of £100 stock, £70. By another party—the landholders, I am accused of wishing to give the lands of the country to the stockholders, and it is more than hinted at that I have an interested view in making the proposal.[74]

Ricardo was not slow in realizing where the problem lay. It was one thing to have diagnosed the burden of the debt—as far as he was concerned it 'destroyed the equilibrium of prices, occasioned many persons to emigrate to other countries, in order to avoid the burthen of taxation which it entailed, and hung like a mill-stone round the exertion and industry of the country'[75]—but it was quite another to expect that an unrepresentative legislature would ever see any such plan through to its completion:

> The most serious obstacle which I see against the adoption of the plan is the state of representation in the House of Commons, which is such as to afford us no security that if we got rid of the present debt, we should not be plunged into another.[76]

---

[74] *Letter to Trower*, 28 December 1819, 8:147.

[75] *Speeches and Evidence*, 9 June 1819, 5:21. A quite different stand on the prospect of redeeming the national debt was taken by Piercy Ravenstone who declaimed that to 'destroy it could only enter into the head of a cold-blooded and wrong-headed political economist, who, shut up in his closet, lost in abstraction . . . has cast away all sympathy with his fellow-creatures, and with the frenzied zeal of a madman is ever eager to pursue his favourite scheme, reckless of the havoc he is dealing around him, and seeing no way to possible good but through certain evil' (*Thoughts on Funding System*, p. 60).

[76] *Letter to Trower*, 28 December 1819, 8:148. It might be noted that in his essay on *Colony* for the Supplement to the *Encyclopedia Britannica*, James Mill had made a very similar point: 'If it be objected . . . that this propensity of governments to spend may be corrected, we answer, that this is not the present question. Take governments as, with hardly any exception, they have always been (this is a pretty wide experience); and the effect is certain. There is one way to be sure, of preventing the great evil, and preventing it thoroughly. But there is only one. In the constitution of the government, make the interest of the many to have the ascendancy over the interest of the few, and the expence of government will not be large' (p. 264).

Of course, it should not be understood from this statement that there were not also deep theoretical issues at stake in the economic debate over the effects on prosperity of government loan expenditure, for there were. Malthus, for one, had built up an argument (though he was not always as consistent as he might have been) to the effect that if the capital of the country was not always fully employed (a condition which, given his adherence to Say's Law, Ricardo seems to have taken for granted), there would be both scope for a productive contribution of government deficit expenditure to national prosperity, and a positive danger of inducing a contraction of economic activity if the debt were to be annihilated overnight. In a long passage at the end of his *Principles of Political Economy*, Malthus stated that argument with considerable clarity:

> If there could be no sort of difficulty in finding profitable for any amount of capital, provided labour were sufficiently abundant, the way to national wealth, though it might not always be easy, would be quite straight, and our only object need be to save from revenue, and repress unproductive consumers. But, if it appears that the greatest powers of production are rendered comparatively useless without effectual consumption, and that a proper distribution of the produce is as necessary to the continued increase of wealth as the means of producing it, it follows that, in cases of this kind, the question depends upon proportions; and it would be the height of rashness to determine, under all circumstances, that the sudden diminution of the national debt and the reduction of taxation must necessarily tend to increase the national wealth, and provide employment for the labouring classes.[77]

[77] *Principles of Political Economy*, p. 411. The analytical problem with Malthus's argument was that he often seemed to apply this to the long-run equilibrium of the system, whereas his framework of concepts (which included Say's Law) meant that its domain of applicability was restricted to short-run disequilibrium. Some of the consequences of this inconsistency for the robustness of Malthus's argument, and its contribution to Ricardo's victory over Malthus in the theoretical debate (so lamented by Keynes) are examined in more detail in Milgate, *Capital and Employment*, pp. 46–57. Nor should it be forgotten that these underlying theoretical differences were reflected in the diagnosis each gave for the economic difficulties which confronted the economy after the war. Malthus, for his part, thought that loan expenditure had greatly contributed to economic expansion during the war, and attributed the economic downturn to other causes;

In this line of thinking, Malthus was followed by William Blake (not the poet, but a friend of Ricardo who, like him, was a member of the London Geological Society and the Political Economy Club). In 1823 Blake had published *Observations on the Expenditure of Government* in which he had argued that mistake of the orthodox Ricardian view lay in its supposition that 'the whole capital of the country is fully occupied; and, secondly, that there is immediate employment for successive accumulations of capital as it accrues from saving'.[78] To these two names one could also add those of Lauderdale and the Birmingham economist Thomas Attwood.

Nevertheless, despite the existence of alternative views, it would be true to say that at the time Ricardo's opinion represented the conventional wisdom on the subject among the classical economists. McCulloch, for example, wrote a long and unfavourable review of Blake's pamphlet in *The Scotsman* for 12 April 1823, and the teenage John Stuart Mill performed a similar service for the Ricardian orthodoxy in the *Westminster Review* for July 1824.[79] So it was natural enough for Ricardo to have assumed the veracity of his argument; even Trower agreed with him on this point.[80] What stands him apart from the rest of his colleagues, is that he turned to the constitution of political society as the chief obstacle to the adoption of the 'right' policy.

Significantly, Ricardo came to oppose the sinking fund for what appear to have been much the same kinds of reasons; namely, the inadequacy of political controls over its misapplication. Without a democratic polity (and perhaps even with one, a point on which

---

Ricardo denied the former, and attributed the latter (in part, at least) to the burden of taxation imposed by the need to finance such a large debt (see his *Notes on Malthus*, 2:451–52).

[78] *Observations*, p. 54; printed in Ricardo's *Works and Correspondence*, 4:340. Ricardo made extensive notes on Blake which are reproduced in that volume (pp. 327–52). Unlike Malthus, however, Blake seems here to have recognized explicitly that the difficulty arose precisely because new saving might not automatically find its way into investment in the short run (that is, he seems to have seen that it was when it was applied to short-run analysis that Say's Law proved to be inadequate). The only substantial account of Blake's economic work is to be found in *The New Palgrave* entry by Giancarlo De Vivo (1:251–52).

[79] 'War expenditure'. See especially p. 47.

[80] See, for example, Trower's own plan (of 1822) for redeeming the debt in Bonar and Hollander's edition of Ricardo's *Letters to Trower*, pp. 183–85.

Ricardo does not explicitly speculate in this case), there was no guarantee against the use of the sinking fund by the government to finance current public expenditures in a way which, instead of contributing to the repayment of the national debt (the purpose for which the fund was designed), actually acted to increase it. On this point, Ricardo had ample evidence in the behaviour of successive Chancellors of the Exchequer (and in the policies of Vansittart in particular) both during and after the Napoleonic Wars. And he was quick to deploy it in his essay on the funding system for the *Encyclopedia Britannica*.[81] In no small measure this explains why Ricardo became skeptical that there were any benefits to be derived from a sinking fund to deal with the problem of the national debt, arguing that 'no securities can be given by ministers that the sinking fund shall be faithfully devoted to the payment of the debt, and without such securities we should be much better without such a fund'.[82]

By structuring his argument about 'the reasonable part of the country' around a theoretical account of the operation of the market mechanism, by grounding the 'science of politics' on the 'science of political economy' Ricardo's politics and his economics are deeply interwoven. For this reason they are vulnerable precisely at that point. Yet in being vulnerable at its very core, Ricardian politics finds itself in distinguished company. Utilitarian politics itself had to face up to the possibility that its particular account of human nature might be wildly inaccurate; while the older, elitist politics of civic virtue might well be accused of inventing a no more viable alternative in its conception of the moral characteristics of the ruling classes.

Be that as it may, Ricardo's arguments clearly led him to embrace a numerically expansive conception of the reasonable part of

---

[81] See *Funding System*, 4:152 et seq. See also the discussion of the Tory financial policy in the immediate post-war years in Boyd Hilton's *Corn, Cash, Commerce* (pp. 33–35), where it is argued that Vansittart 'abused the sinking fund' (p. 33) to finance current expenditures on public services. Sidney Buxton was rather more blunt on the subject of Vansittart; deploying Dr. Johnson's words, he described him as a man with a 'mind as narrow as a vinegar cruet' (*Finance and Politics*, 1:15). Ricardo himself seems to have been well aware of Vansittart's propensity in this direction; see his speech in the House of Commons, 6 March 1821 (5:79–80).

[82] *Funding System*, 4:196.

the country; and from this he was led to the advocacy of extensive democratic participation in the political process under the actual conditions which then prevailed in Britain. Of course, his next task was to provide an account of the degree of political stability a new constitutional arrangement of this kind would exhibit. But before turning to Ricardo's argument on that score, it will be instructive to dwell for a moment on the manner in which Ricardo went about deciding upon who, if anyone, should be excluded from the electoral franchise. For Ricardo did not naïvely employ the conceptual category 'the reasonable part of the country' simply to mean everybody, without exception. Potentially, of course, it opens up his politics to universal suffrage, but theoretically there was a principle of exclusion.

✣ CHAPTER FOUR ✣

The Principle of Exclusion

IN RECOMMENDATIONS concerning the appropriate organization of a democratic polity—philosophic-radical, Ricardian, or otherwise—the demand for universal suffrage is never meant to be taken literally. Except, perhaps, in the most pure of cases, there is always a qualification to be met.[1] The People, in whose name political authority is exercised, and upon whose sanction its continued legitimacy is made to depend, are, in this sense, an artificial entity. Some are always excluded. Leaving aside the question of the enfranchisement of women, a subject on which Ricardo said nothing,[2] it is clear from what we have already said that Ricardo's electorate was extensive. To begin with, the most familiar exclusionary principle other than gender—namely, social class—had already been called into question by Ricardo in the context of his delineation of the reasonable part of the country. However, these were not the only grounds on which exclusion from the political nation was mandated in Britain at the time. Another was religion.

In the early decades of the nineteenth century, of course, the debate over religious toleration was played out largely in the con-

[1] Ricardo is no exception, and the fact that he never endorsed universality should in no way diminish the assessment of his commitment or contribution to democratic thought in the early nineteenth century. For his specific reservations about universal suffrage, see *Works and Correspondence* 5:29, 45, 502; 7:270, 360, 369–70; 8:99, 107, 129. On his qualified support for a plan of household suffrage, see *Works and Correspondence*, 5:473, 485; 7:273 & n.

[2] Perhaps it would be better to say 'almost nothing'. For Ricardo stated his support for Sir Samuel Romilly's scheme for universal *household* suffrage in 1818 (*Letter to Trower*, 27 June 1818, 7:273); a scheme modelled on the existing scot-and-lot franchise in Westminster. Romilly, a moderate Whig reformer and successively member for Queenborough, Wareham and Arundel, was returned for Westminster (along with the radical Sir Francis Burdett) in 1818. To the extent that household suffrage gave the vote only to a representative of the whole, it might be said that Ricardo's support for it placed him squarely in the camp of James Mill. However, this must remain mere speculation, since unlike Mill, Ricardo never explicitly claimed that the interests of women were 'virtually' represented by their spouses.

text of the Catholic Question. With the Roman Catholic community deprived of political liberties, enjoying neither the franchise nor the right to occupy a seat in either House of Parliament, and being severely disadvantaged in the civil sphere as well, the issue of Catholic emancipation was high on the agenda of parliamentary reformers. Although Non-Conforming and Dissenting protestant sects had originally laboured under many of the same civil disabilities, the eighteenth century had witnessed a gradual relaxation in both the letter and the application of the laws which curtailed their civil liberties.

The newer evangelical protestant sects, for example, had found ways around the Corporation and Test Acts, under which a whole array of military, civil, and political offices were closed to those who refused to swear an oath rejecting the authority of the See of Rome and to take the Sacrament according to the rites of the Church of England. The expedient of occasional conformity, of taking communion in the Anglican form only to return to one's own congregation thereafter (outlawed in 1719), was sufficiently widespread by the end of the eighteenth century as to have seen parliament adopt the convention of passing yearly Indemnity Bills which issued a blanket pardon for all breaches of the 1719 Act that had taken place in the previous year.[3] Although such a deception may have weighed heavily on the conscience of many a dissenter who was forced to adopt it, it did not amount to apostasy as it would have done for practising Catholics. Furthermore, the Toleration Act of 1689 had already formally expanded the civil rights of dissenting protestants by legalizing all assemblies at which the form of worship did not follow the liturgy of the Church of

[3] Ricardo himself had a direct encounter with the Test Act when (late in 1817) he found his name to be second on the list of nominees for the office of High Sheriff of Gloucestershire for 1818. In a letter to Malthus he wrote: 'As Col. Berkeley, the first named, will in all probability be excused on account of his intended application to the House of Lords for the Peerage . . . I shall no doubt be selected' (Letter to Malthus, 16 December 1817, 7:223–24). This office was subject to the provisions of the Test Act, and Ricardo instructed his lawyers to seek an opinion as to what course of action should be followed. There were two options: to seek exemption under the Toleration Act, or to rely on the annual Act of Indemnity for violations against the Test Act. The lawyers favoured the first as the safest course, but were confident that the annual Act of Indemnity would be sufficient. (See the account given by Sraffa in Works and Correspondence 10:42–43.)

England provided only that a declaratory oath be signed affirming the participant's protestantism, his repudiation of Papal authority, including a denial of the doctrine of Transubstantiation.[4]

For Roman Catholics, as will be perfectly clear, the case was quite different. For them, the Toleration Act was not tolerant, and there were no practical expedients by which the Corporation and Test Acts could be circumvented (save conversion) in order to facilitate political participation. Even the proposal issuing from some of their own number, that British Catholics would agree to limit the domain of Papal authority to spiritual matters in return for political and civil emancipation, fell on deaf ears—and this only partly because the dividing line between matters spiritual and matters temporal was difficult to draw. No other single religious community, with the exception of the Jews, was similarly disadvantaged. 'Church of Englandism', as Bentham dubbed it, was dominant.

> A Catholic could be a barrister but he could not be a judge of a High Court. In Great Britain he neither possessed the franchise nor could he hold even a subordinate rank in the Army or Navy. Nowhere in the United Kingdom had he the right to command a regiment or a vessel of the line, to occupy a post in the administration, to be elected to the Commons, to take his seat in the Lords.[5]

The party lines on the Catholic Question were well-enough established (though they were not without their usual quirks) by the time Ricardo entered politics. When the Tories, under Lord Liverpool, had (in 1812) determined, in Thomas Creevy's words, 'not to oppose the Catholic question as a Governmental measure' but rather to allow everyone 'to do as he pleases',[6] they had effectively determined not to sponsor the measure. The implications of this strategy were not lost on the opposition side. In a speech on the Prince Regent's Address at the opening of Parliament in 1819, Henry Parnell observed that 'the situation of the Catholics of Ire-

---

[4] James Mill was disparaging in his account of such oath-swearing: 'We need not allude to the daily use of fiscal oaths, and theological oaths, to be reminded of the perfect callousness with which false swearing is practised and regarded' ('The ballot', p. 34).

[5] Elie Halévy, *History of the English People*, 1:474.

[6] *Letter to Mrs. Creevy*, 9 June 1812, in Maxwell (ed.), *The Creevy Papers* 1:166.

land had been, as usual, wholly omitted'; and he went on to sum up the situation quite succinctly:

> To adopt the course that these occasional friends of the question pursued, was to leave the question to time and chance to work some, at present not foreseen, circumstances, to secure its final settlement.[7]

Even as late as 1829 in the debate over the Catholic Emancipation Act, Tory Ultras, like Lord Eldon, were prepared to declare their preference for death over the possibility of having to 'awake to the reflection, that I had consented to an act, which stamped me as a violator of my solemn oath, a traitor to my church, and a traitor to the constitution'.[8]

Tory Liberals, on the other hand, were divided. Some, like Peel, were opposed to emancipation. In Peel's case this was partly due to his earlier political involvement in the Irish question. Others, however, like Canning and Huskisson, were more in the mould of Pitt and Castlereagh[9] who had been (if only for pragmatic reasons) sympathetic to the cause at the beginning of the century.[10] The closeness of the parallel may be measured, perhaps, by the fact that in 1813 Canning had added to the draft of a proposed Catholic Emancipation Bill (which failed to gain the assent of the House) a clause establishing a Board of Commissioners to scrutinize all nominations to Catholic bishoprics that was similar in form to an arrangement Castlereagh had secretly concluded back in 1799. But Tory Liberals were to remain a minority faction until the middle of the 1820s and, in any case, they could not be expected to break ranks if it jeopardized their patronage or meant

---

[7] *Hansard* 39:64.

[8] From the *Hansard* report of his speech of 10 April 1829 as reproduced in Black's *British Politics*, p. 46. On being accused of a certain inconsistency in taking this stand (inasmuch as he had never, it seems, actually entered a church), Brougham reports that Lord Eldon apparently replied that his support for the Church of England was more 'a buttress which was placed outside' (*Historical Sketches* 2:66n).

[9] See Leslie Stephen, *The English Utilitarians*, 2:59.

[10] In 1800 Pitt had planned to sweeten the bitter pill of the Union of Great Britain and Ireland with a measure of Catholic emancipation and Castlereagh had been involved in secret talks with ten bishops in an effort to secure Catholic agreement to a procedure whereby the British Government would be allowed to vet the names of nominees for bishoprics before they were forwarded to Rome.

compromising the government in the country.[11] What is more, always lurking just behind the Catholic Question was the Irish Question; and this was a matter on which Tory opinion was far more rigid and homogeneous.

The Whigs, for their part, were uniformly for toleration. Even before the first decade of the new century had passed, the Whigs had become, as Halévy put it, the party of Catholic emancipation.[12] This, despite the factionalism that characterized the Whigs at the time. This given, perhaps the more interesting feature of the Whig toleration platform at the time was its character rather than its content. It lacked altogether the moral zeal with which, in other areas, the Whig platform is sometimes said to have been stamped. Brougham, for example, who spoke on the subject in the early 1820s with regularity, seems to have found in the Catholic Question more an opportunity for making the telling party-politi-

[11] The electoral appeal of the toleration platform raises interesting but complicated issues (as, indeed, does the more general question of the relation between party politics and religious affiliation); and this is not the place to go into it. It is clear, however, that from an electoral standpoint the spread of Evangelicalism and Methodist 'revivalism' into dissenting protestant circles had meant that by the early part of the nineteenth century the Whigs could no longer take for granted the support they had enjoyed from that part of the Christian community for the better part of a century. The rationalism of the old sects was steadily giving way to the emotionalism of the new. And the essentially conservative character of the politics of some of these newer sects (witness the anti-Jacobin pronouncements of Wesley and the almost wholly Tory membership of the Clapham Evangelical sect—the 'Party of the Saints'—led by William Wilberforce and including economist Henry Thornton), together with their anti-Catholic rhetoric, was not lost on mainstream Tory party strategists; to the extent that at the general election in 1807 a 'No-Popery' theme was woven into the Tory campaign. An interesting discussion of the changing character of the attitude of the Tories to the activities of these Methodist sects can be found in Elie Halévy's *History of the English People* (1:426–29).

[12] *History of the English People* 1:429. As to the source and basis of this commitment to freedom of worship, there is greater divergence of opinion. For some, it is simply further proof of that apparently infallible Whig instinct to take up the moral high ground in the battle between freedom and the forces of darkness. To others, however, the spur behind Whig toleration was the existence of very real geo-political threats (not least, from Napoleon just across the Channel). Leslie Stephen also claimed that while the typical Whig 'would not risk the country for the sake of the church', nevertheless the church was a part of a balanced constitutional arrangement and was, as such, entitled 'to be guarded from the rude assaults of the Radical reformer' (*The English Utilitarians* 2:60).

cal point against the Tories, rather than a chance for making a case in principle. His most famous parliamentary clash with Canning in 1823, for instance, which saw him accuse Canning of providing a specimen of the most 'monstrous truckling for the purpose of obtaining office that the whole history of political tergiversation could furnish' (and which saw both men escourted from the House by the sergeant at arms), seems to be a case in point.[13]

During most of Ricardo's career, of course, the Radicals could scarcely be said to have been represented in parliament at all.[14] Other than Ricardo himself, what parliamentary voice they had was raised through Francis Burdett,[15] Joseph Hume,[16] and John Cam Hobhouse. Hume had been a school friend of James Mill who, although starting his parliamentary career as a Tory (for Weymouth) in 1812, was returned for Aberdeen in 1818 as a reformer.

---

[13] There is an informative discussion of Brougham's position in this regard in Hawes's *Henry Brougham*, pp. 184–88. As Hawes puts it: 'One gets the impression in reading his speeches on the Catholic claims that they are rather in support of liberal legislation in general, and incidently an excellent party weapon, than the expression of urgent personal conviction' (p. 186). A firsthand lesson in the importance to the Whigs of the Catholic Question as a weapon of party politics may be gleaned from a reading of *The Creevy Papers* both for the early months of 1823 and for those surrounding Catholic Emancipation itself in 1829.

[14] Cobbett thought otherwise; Westminster was just another rotten borough as far as he was concerned.

[15] Burdett had entered the Commons in 1796 as the member for Boroughbridge (a seat he had purchased from the Duke of Newcastle). In 1807 he was returned for Westminster (Francis Place having been his campaign manager) and he remained as one of its representatives until his death in 1837; this despite (or perhaps because of) his having been committed to the Tower on a vote by the House of Commons for a breach of privilege in 1810 for publishing a speech he had made on freedom of discussion in Cobbett's *Political Register*. However, according to M. W. Patterson, Burdett was, throughout his life, 'half-Radical, half-Tory' but never in any sense a Whig. Thus, with the passage of the Reform Bill, Burdett's 'greatest political aim' was achieved, and his long-term associations with the Radicals dissolved as he moved to embrace a regenerated Toryism under Peel. In part, as Patterson suggests, Burdett's change of poltical alignments reflected his later desire 'to protect property and to preserve national institutions' and his belief that the destruction of any one form of property might incite the destruction of all forms (*Sir Francis Burdett and His Times (1770–1844)*, pp. 627–29).

[16] Ricardo described him as 'a most useful member of parliament,—always at his post and governed I believe by an ardent desire to be useful to his country' (*Letter to Trower*, 21 July 1820, 8:210).

Burdett (for Westminster), being of a character that was mercurial to a fault, was less predictable an ally than many of the radicals might have wished for. John Cam Hobhouse (also for Westminster) joined the faction in 1820, but neither he nor Burdett were highly regarded by the Radicals outside parliament for the consistency of their performance within it. The extent of the gap that had grown up between them and certain segments of the Radical constituency may be gauged by Francis Place's observation (made in 1826) that 'Burdett and Hobhouse are little if any better than mere drawling Whigs'.[17] Nevertheless, both Burdett and Hobhouse supported Catholic emancipation, Burdett repeatedly introducing petitions and motions on the question in the mid 1820s; and Hume 'every year asked Parliament to disendow at least partially the Church of Ireland'.[18]

For extra-parliamentary philosophical radicals, it was, not surprisingly, Bentham who was the oracle. Religion, by which Bentham meant belief in a Supreme Being and in a future state, was akin to despotism. It was harmful to the individual and to society. While one might debate whether these opinions were atheistic or not, that they were irreligious there can be no doubt. More to the point, however, Bentham had long been the advocate not just of religious toleration, but also of the disestablishment of the Church of England. In this way, he had transformed the Catholic Question. Whereas in other circles the debate focused on the narrower matter of securing a degree of political inclusion for adherents of the Church of Rome, in Benthamite circles it was used to address the much broader goal of securing nothing less than the complete separation of church and state. In this, of course, Bentham was followed by James Mill. Even if Elie Halévy was correct to wonder whether the radicals (and he singled out Hume's performances in the House of Commons in particular) helped or hindered the cause of Catholic emancipation,[19] there can be no doubt that they supported it.

---

[17] Quoted by Graham Wallas in his *Life of Francis Place*, p. 153. Interestingly, on the declaration of the results of the Westminster election in the summer of 1818, when Burdett and Samuel Romilly were returned, Ricardo wrote to Malthus that he thought Burdett to be 'a consistent man' (*Letter to Malthus*, 24 June 1818, 7:270).

[18] Halévy, *History of the English People*, 2:219.

[19] Ibid.

At the most general level, Ricardo's views on religious toleration seem to have been the standard fare of philosophical radicalism. Though articulated in less colourful language than anything employed by Bentham, who had grown up as a child of David Hume, Ricardo objected to all forms of discrimination grounded on religious affiliation. He voiced such opinions repeatedly in the House of Commons. Speaking in support of a petition for the release of Mary Ann Carlile who had been gaoled for blasphemous libel for selling works by Thomas Paine,[20] Ricardo had argued that since all 'religious opinions, however absurd and extravagant, might be conscientiously believed by some individuals' it was unacceptable that one man should by law be permitted 'to set up his ideas on the subject as the criterion from which no other was to be allowed to differ with impunity'. Instead, Ricardo maintained that a 'fair and free discussion ought to be allowed on all religious topics'.[21]

Indeed, it would seem to have been the case that for Ricardo even the complete absence of any religious belief whatsoever provided no ground for disqualification from political citizenship. Just such an argument appears to lie behind his speech to the House of Commons in July 1823 in support of a petition for free discussion introduced by Joseph Hume. *Hansard* reported that Ricardo 'firmly believed in the possibility of a man's being very honest for all social purposes and essential obligations of the community in which he lived, and still not assenting to the belief of a future state'.[22]

[20] Ms. Carlile, sister of the well-known radical pamphleteer, bookseller, and the publisher of Paine's *Age of Reason* in England, Richard Carlile, was prosecuted by the Society for the Suppression of Vice for selling a copy of *An Appendix to the Theological Works of Thomas Paine*. Her sentence had been for a year's imprisonment and a fine of £500. If on the expiry of the year the fine remained unpaid, the guilty party was to remain in prison until the fine was discharged. The year had been served, but the fine was still outstanding, and a petition had come before the House of Commons for her release (see Sraffa's editorial annotations in *Works and Correspondence*, 5:277).

[21] *Speeches and Evidence*, 26 March 1823, 5:280.

[22] Ibid., 1 July 1823, 5:327. A little incident surrounding this speech bears recording. In this speech Ricardo had gone on to cite the case of Robert Owen, asking: 'Why, then, was such a man (for by the law he was) to be excluded from the pale of legal credibility'? (5:328). This led another member (Mr. Money) to chide Ricardo, saying that Owen had communicated to him the falsity of Ricardo's claim. Ricardo's defence against the charge on the floor of the House was rather feeble. He was not amused. It seems that Ricardo had himself obtained Owen's

Privately, however, Ricardo was prepared to be much more explicit on the matter. In a letter to Isaac Goldsmid, the campaigner for Jewish emancipation who had registered his admiration of Ricardo's speech on the Mary Ann Carlile petition, Ricardo stated that he was quite prepared to 'carry my principles of toleration very far'; so far, indeed, that on the question of political exclusion he did not 'know how, or why any line should be drawn, and am prepared to maintain that we have no more justifiable ground for shutting the mouth of an Atheist than that of any other man'.[23] Years earlier, in commenting to Trower on the decision of John Bird Sumner (later to become the Archbishop of Canterbury) to abandon political economy for theology, Ricardo allowed himself a playful reflection: '[w]hether in this latter pursuit he will have an equal chance of benefiting mankind, as in the former, I have great doubts, or rather I have no doubt at all'.[24]

On the specific question of Catholic emancipation, Ricardo did not speak in Parliament, but was very clear in his correspondence. In 1820 he wrote to Trower that while he did not expect much reform from the new ministry, he was at least confident that 'we may probably find men who will remove the disabilities from the Roman catholics'.[25] In 1821, again to Trower, he reported that William Plunkett (the member for Trinity College, Dublin) had made a 'very fine' speech in support of a motion for the establishment of a committee to examine the claims of Irish Catholics, adding that he 'should not see much to regret if Ireland had a catholic establishment, in the same way as Scotland has a presbyterian one'.[26] Plunkett's motion passed the Commons but was defeated in the Lords, at which time Ricardo wrote again to Trower: '[T]he catholic bill is lost. I am sorry for it, though I cannot but think it is

consent to the remark before he had made it, and was understandably annoyed at his subsequent disavowal of it; but he refused to reveal the exchange in his reply (see the editorial annotations in *Speeches and Evidence* 5:331n.1, for more of the details).

[23] *Letter to Goldsmid*, 4 April 1823, 9:278.

[24] *Letter to Trower*, 26 January 1818, 7:248. Interestingly enough, once installed as Archbishop of Canterbury in 1848, Sumner became 'a consistent opponent of the bill for removing Jewish disabilities' (see *Dictionary of National Biography*).

[25] *Letter to Trower*, 26 November 1820, 8:304.

[26] Ibid., 2 March 1821, 8:350–51.

only delayed'.[27] The curious absence of Ricardo's name from the published list of the division on Plunkett's motion, which prompted Edwin Cannan to speculate that perhaps Ricardo had abstained under pressure from Lord Portarlington[28] (at whose pleasure he occupied his parliamentary seat), seems rather to have been an error.[29]

There is an addendum to be made to the above account of Ricardo's radical opinions on the subject of religion. William Wilberforce, who also spoke in the debate over the petition on behalf of Mary Ann Carlile to which Ricardo had contributed (and with whom, on the subject of toleration, Ricardo was again to cross swords in the House of Commons in July 1823), sarcastically remarked that Ricardo had 'seemed to carry into more weighty matters those principles of free trade which he had so successfully expounded'.[30] Furthermore, after this debate Wilberforce made an entry in his diary (in reference to Ricardo) to the effect that while he 'had hoped that [__] had become a Christian', he could now see that 'he has only ceased to be a Jew'.[31] This episode merits attention because it highlights an important, and not always unspoken, consequence for the reception of Ricardo's views of his family background as the son of a Sephardic Jew. For an anti-Semitic theme in commentary on Ricardo has not been the exclusive preserve of his political opponents. Walter Bagehot, as we have already seen, indulged in it. Even Alfred Marshall, no small admirer of Ricardo, remarked on his un-Englishness, and attributed an alleged 'bias towards the abstract calculations connected with the trade of money dealing' to Ricardo's 'Semitic origin'.[32]

We mention these comments because they speak quite directly to the question of the *reception* of those opinions. What the prevalence of this kind of stereotyping confirms (apart, of course, from

[27] Ibid., 21 April 1821, 8:369.

[28] Noticing this, Cannan enquired: 'Can it have been due to some compact with the power which gave him his seat for Portarlington?' ('Ricardo in parliament', 1:254).

[29] See Sraffa's editorial remarks on this subject in *Works and Correspondence*, 5:xxii–xxiii.

[30] These remarks are reported in Sraffa's editorial annotations to this speech in ibid., p. 280n.1.

[31] Ibid.

[32] *Principles of Economics*, p. 629n.1. (Marshall also cites Bagehot's opinion in this passage.)

the particular prejudices of its propagators), is Ricardo's status as an outsider. This was something Ricardo was well aware of:

> It appears to me a disgrace to the age we live in, that a part of the inhabitants of this country are still suffering under disabilities imposed upon them in a less enlightened time. The jews have most reason to complain, for they are frequently reproached for the dishonesty, which is the natural effect of the political degradation in which they are kept.[33]

Whether or not this outsider status played any part in shaping Ricardo's ability to take an independent and distinctively more objective stance on constitutional reform than either Mill or Bentham, one can only speculate. However, what all of this makes very clear is that one must look beyond the qualifications of religion or class to unearth Ricardo's principle of exclusion.

On the question of whether gender (namely, being a woman) ought to disqualify one from citizenship or not, Ricardo, as we have already had cause to remark, said nothing specific. To be sure, from the practical reforms to which he offered his not inconsiderable support, it does seem clear that he was much closer to James Mill on this particular subject than he was either to Bentham, or, for that matter, to John Stuart Mill. Indeed, there is just no evidence at all to suggest that Ricardo departed in any significant way from the established position on women's suffrage that was entertained in the circles in which he moved. This was characterized by a sort of paternalism which, if not entirely benign, was perhaps more advanced than that entertained in certain other radical quarters. It should not be forgotten that, at the time, there were radicals who actually thought that Bentham's proposal for the enfranchisement of women did little more than allow ridicule to be heaped onto the 'serious' cause of parliamentary reform. Probably the most generous thing that could be said of Ricardo, therefore, is that the issue of gender equality did not enter prominently in his politics. Of course, the fact that the criterion which Ricardo invariably applied to determine the question of citizenship, full participation in economic life, was one that was later to be invoked to support the right of women to vote, is not without its own in-

---

[33] *Letter to Goldsmid*, 4 April 1823, 9:278.

terest. Equally, it is not indicative that Ricardo himself applied it in this way.

Ricardo's formal concession that some exclusionary principle was required appeared initially in the context of his exchanges with Trower who, as we have seen, was happy enough to exclude all those already excluded. Ricardo objected to this intransigence in the following terms:

> The most you can require of the friends of reform is the right to challenge such electors as are *without the necessary qualifications.* Now this right I freely yield to you; show the *sinister interest,* or the probability of a bad choice, and I will consent to deprive the individual to whom they attach of the right of electing members.[34]

The question remains, however, as to what exactly the 'necessary qualifications' were to be. When Ricardo first turned his attention to this subject (in the spring of 1818) his opinions, though still not fully formed, seem to have been leaning towards the notion that some form of property qualification might provide the answer as to the extent of the franchise. Of course, it is hardly surprising that this is where Ricardo should first have looked, since the existing legislation (with its famous 40/- freeholder and scot-and-lot constituencies) had couched the electoral qualification in just that way. Thus, we find him writing to Trower in March 1818 in the following terms:

> If the suffrage is not universal there can be no danger of anarchy. A man with a very small property can have no wish for confusion if he be actuated by those motives which have always been found to influence mankind.[35]

Given these statements, it is scarcely surprising that at this time, although declaring himself convinced by Bentham's *Plan of Parliamentary Reform,* Ricardo also countenanced the possibility that Bentham had gone a little too far.[36] Moreover, at about the same time he actually suggested to Malthus that the reports he had received of Sir James Mackintosh's opinions on parliamentary reform had led him to the conclusion that he did not think that he and

[34] *Letter to Trower,* 2 November 1818, 7:321.
[35] Ibid., 22 March 1818, 7:261.
[36] Ibid., p. 260.

Mackintosh would 'be so much opposed'.[37] As it was to transpire, however, these reports turned out to be drastically in error. In December 1818 Mackintosh came out in the *Edinburgh Review* against everything Bentham had said. Indeed, in no small measure James Mill's essay on *Government* for the Supplement to the *Encyclopedia Britannica* can be understood as the Radicals' response. Soon, too, Ricardo's thinking began to change; and so rapidly that by the winter of 1818 his position had crystallized.

According to that more considered opinion, the ownership of property did not now provide the grounds upon which individuals were seen to qualify for citizenship. Instead, Ricardo proposed that the exclusionary line was to be drawn just above those who could be shown to 'have an interest' in overthrowing the régime of private property itself:

> You call upon me to 'limit the right of voting at Elections to such persons who by their education have the ability to decide correctly' and then you would have fewer objections to reform. In other words you would require security for a good choice of representatives and this is precisely what I want. If I cannot obtain it without limiting the elective franchise to the very narrowest bounds, I would so limit it; but I am persuaded that we should most securely get our object, and should be less exposed to hazards of a different kind, by extending the elective franchise,—not indeed universally to all people, but to that part of them which cannot be supposed to have any interest in overturning the rights of property.[38]

By settling on only those social attachments that might flow from a commitment to a form of economic organization based on private ownership, Ricardo's argument was the bearer of many of the most familiar themes of early philosophic-radical thinking (and, for that matter, of its later variants as well). Of course, the general idea that some shared attachments were essential to the stability of the political community was, on its own, scarcely sufficient to distinguish between any of the camps in the great debate over parliamentary reform; on that subject they were in near unanimous agreement. What counted was not just that political society should be permeated by shared attachments. Rather, everything hinged

[37] *Letter to Malthus*, 25 May 1818, 7:263.
[38] *Letter to Trower*, 20 December 1818, 7:370.

upon exactly what commitments were felt to be indispensable to it, and in which segments of society those sentiments might safely be thought to have resided. On these more decisive questions, Ricardo's thinking was distinctive. By construing the legitimate demands that could be made of citizens so minimally (and so early), Ricardo's argument opened up the franchise to a potentially far greater number of individuals than was the case with most of his philosophic-radical friends at the time; save Bentham. When taken in conjunction with his clear articulation of the reasonable part of the country as those individuals actively participating in economic life, it is evident that Ricardo had chosen to identify the standards of political participation with no more (but no less) than those of involvement in modern market activity. In the final analysis, then, it would appear to have been from this simple equation that Ricardo was led to comprehend the interests of all classes in society, including those of the mass of ordinary labourers, as being congruent with the preservation and perpetuation of a capitalistic organization of material economic life.

Missing are all remnants of old-fashioned, eighteenth-century notions of civic virtue as a pre-requisite to citizenship. Missing, too, is any trace of the modified version of the doctrine of virtual representation promulgated by Whig reformers like Mackintosh, Jeffrey, or Russell. More significant than this, however, is the fact that missing also is any easy and comfortable identification of the morality of the middling ranks of society with that required for political participation. That theme, which continued to gain expression in the speculations of James Mill, is entirely absent from Ricardo's argument.

In his *Observations on Parliamentary Reform*, Ricardo made the case for exclusion in the very same terms he had adduced in his exchanges with Trower:

> So essential does it appear to me, to the cause of good government, that the rights of property should be held sacred, that I would agree to deprive those of the elective franchise against whom it could justly be alleged that they considered it their interest to invade them.[39]

[39] *Parliamentary Reform*, 5:500–501. It is worth re-stating that this test for electoral qualification had nothing to do with whether one was for or against the constitutional monarchy (*Letter to Trower*, 2 November 1818, 7:320); that is, repub-

Thus, it is to the 'security of property', 'that principle which should ever be held sacred',[40] rather than to the ownership of that property, that Ricardo would direct us for the principle of exclusion. For Ricardo, then, threats to the security of the political nation could not be expected to come simply from those who had no property, but only from those who refused to respect it. To those who feared the consequences of enfranchising the propertyless, Ricardo replied:

> But in fact it can only be amongst the most needy in the community that such opinions can be entertained . . . and it may be doubted whether any large number of even the lowest would, if they could, promote a division of property. It is the bugbear by which the corrupt always endeavour to rally those who have property to lose around them.[41]

At this point, it is worth commenting on the contrast between the mode of argumentation Ricardo deployed on the question of property qualifications and that adopted by James Mill. For although both arrived at essentially the same conclusion as to the inefficacy of a property qualification, the route they traversed to get there seems to have been quite different. Indeed, when one compares the two, it is difficult not to find some substance in Ricardo's claim to have been 'a reformer on principle',[42] while at the same time sympathizing with those (and there have been not a few of them[43]) who have seen in Mill's manner of argumentation the lawyer's cast of mind. Having to his own satisfaction deduced (from the principle of utility) that representative democracy was the *only* means of securing good government,[44] Mill's argument on the property question runs as follows. First, take a high qualification; this must be rejected because it would give us just another form of aristocratic or oligarchic government. Next, consider a low qual-

---

lican sentiments were no grounds for disqualification (recall the discussion of this point in chapter 1 above).

[40] *Principles*, 1:204.

[41] *Parliamentary Reform*, 5:501.

[42] *Letter to Trower*, 30 January 1823, 9:267.

[43] See, for example, Halévy, *Philosophic Radicalism*, p. 421 and Plamenatz, *The English Utilitarians*, p. 106.

[44] To highlight the point, Mill entitled the sixth section of *Government* 'In the Representative System *alone* the Securities for good Government are to be found' (p. 16, italics added).

ification; this, too, must be rejected. A 'very low qualification is of no use, as affording no security for a good choice beyond that which would exist if no pecuniary qualification was required',[45] since the votes of the propertyless would be so few as not to disturb the interest of the 'community'. 'Therefore' no property qualification was necessary to the security of good government.

Nor is this the only way in which Mill's formulation of the question of electoral qualification differs from Ricardo. In casting his philosopher's eye across the list of names of potential electors, Mill concocts an interesting exclusionary criterion which, for want of a better label, we have previously characterized as a new virtualism. 'One thing is pretty clear', he asserts, this is 'that all those whose interests are indisputably included in those of other individuals, may be struck off without inconvenience'.[46] It is thanks to this particular criterion, that women and children (with the age of forty apparently being Mill's preferred boundary between minority and majority[47]) are struck off Mill's electoral register.

There are several things that need to be said about this argument. In the first place, confining ourselves to matters of logic for the moment, Mill's conclusion is quite inconsistent with the utilitarian argument upon which it is supposed to be based. We have already had cause to remark that the application of utility theory to any problem of choice (political, economic, or otherwise) requires (among other things) the assumption that agents possess the capacity to choose: namely, that they have full information as to the possibilities and consequences of their actions. Models of rational self-interest, in other words, assume not just rationality but also knowledge. When addressing the problem of who should be excluded from the electoral register, it is therefore logical to check that each of these conditions are met by voters. Thus, in certain parts of the essay on *Government*, as we have noticed, Mill is led, quite consistently, to advance education as a criterion against which to judge the suitability of electors. However, the idea that when one agent's interests are 'included' in another's (whatever

[45] *Government*, p. 22.

[46] Ibid., p. 21.

[47] Ibid., p. 22. The supposed security to good government afforded by this qualification is, according to Mill, that 'men of forty have a deep interest in the welfare of the younger men'.

that might mean),[48] utility theory mandates our excluding one or other of them is quite false. Under a simple majority-rule voting procedure, in a society that consisted of more than two individuals, even if a woman whose interests were supposedly 'included' in those of some other man had *identical* preferences to that man,[49] political choice would in general fail to satisfy Mill's utilitarian criterion of the greatest aggregate utility.[50]

Given James Mill's argument on this point, it is ironic that the old adage 'like father, like son' fails so conspicuously in this case to apply to the contributions of John Stuart Mill to the campaign for women's suffrage. For while the reasoning that led James Mill to disenfranchise women and children was fundamentally flawed, that which led his son to campaign for the enfranchisement of women while retaining adult suffrage (of course, the younger Mill would disenfranchise only real children) was, logically speaking, watertight.

Against this, however, it has to be said that when one actually pauses for a moment to consider just how many of 'the many' would have been enfranchised under James Mill's suggested scheme (that is, if one makes a rough estimate of the number of names that would appear on his electoral register for Great Britain and Ireland), the result turns out to be surprising; despite the problematic logic of the whole argument and the very limited conception of political equality it seems to embrace. Taking the demographic profile for Great Britain and Ireland for 1820, the year Mill's essay appeared, the number of males aged forty or above was approximately 2.1 million; that is, 10 percent of a total popu-

[48] Whether one should be prepared to assume this is invariably the case for husbands and wives, and for parents and children, as Mill seems to do, is quite another matter.

[49] Of course, there is no reason to expect this to be the case, and if it is not, then the implications for logic of Mill's argument are even more damaging than in the case where it is. It might well be noticed here that a famous attack on Mill's argument about disenfranchising women, namely, that contained in William Thompson's *An Appeal of One-Half the Human Race, Women, Against the Pretensions of the Other Half, Men*, relied almost entirely on establishing the absence of an identity of interest between the two.

[50] William Thomas discusses Mill's argument for the disenfranchisement of women and children on these grounds, but fails to notice its logical inconsistency (*Philosophic Radicals*, p. 128). The same is true of Gregory Claeys in *Citizens and Saints* (p. 173).

lation of about 21 million.[51] Assuming that the existing electorate numbered approximately five hundred thousand adult males,[52] had all of Mill's old men been enfranchised, the scheme would have witnessed an increase of the electoral franchise by a factor of four.

Some appreciation of the kind of adjustment in the electoral franchise the adoption of Mill's scheme would have entailed can be gauged by recalling that when parliamentary reform actually did come in 1832, Lord John Russell estimated that if enacted his Bill would add about half a million voters to the electoral rolls of a kingdom of some twenty-four million inhabitants[53] (and this, it should be emphasised, under a 'man of property' franchise, where one attained majority status at age twenty-one not forty). Had this estimate been accurate, the First Reform Bill would have roughly doubled the existing electoral franchise. As it turned out, the net addition to the franchise was a little over three hundred thousand.[54] The comparative statistics, however, tell only part of the story of the distance which separated the Whig and Radical reformers of the day. It has to be remembered that for most of the Whig reformers the First Reform Bill stood at the end of the road to democracy, while for the Radicals it marked only its beginning. Thus, for example, as Home Secretary in Lord Melbourne's cabinet, Lord John Russell declared at the opening of Parliament after the 1837 general election (in the speech which earned for him in radical circles the nickname 'Finality Jack'[55]) that the wide scope of the constitutional re-adjustment worked by the First Reform Bill was acceded to by his Whig colleagues precisely because it was meant to be final. On the eve of the decade of the Chartists, which was so to alter the political landscape of Britain, it is remarkable that the distance thought left to be covered after the First Reform Bill was believed to be negligible by the political leadership of the day.

[51] See Mitchell's *British Historical Statistics*, Table I.2, pp. 9–10 and Pope's *Atlas*, Table 6.2, p. 136.

[52] See Cook and Stevenson, *Historical Facts*, pp. 54–59. This is probably an overestimate.

[53] See his speech in the House of Commons, 1 March 1831, as reprinted in Eugene Black's *British Politics*, p. 70.

[54] See Halévy's *History of The English People*, 3:27n.5.

[55] See Spencer Walpole's *Life of Lord John Russell*, 1:289–90 and Wallas's *Life of Francis Place*, p. 366.

Nevertheless, while the essay on *Government* was heralded by Mill as a quite unanswerable and generally applicable philosophical argument against aristocracy and in favour of representative democracy (and not just as a practical proposal for increasing the size of the electorate), it is surprising that James Mill's philosophic-radical politics would effectively substitute the constitutional domination of one aristocracy for that of another; one based on age and gender, rather than birth.

The logic which inspired Mill's new virtualism, differs from Ricardo's thinking on the subject of representative government. This fact comes out particularly clearly in a short exchange between the two on the publication of Mill's *History of British India*, where Mill seems to have applied it to determine the mode of government best-suited to the colony. Ricardo had read Mill's book when it appeared in late 1817, and had discussed it in correspondence with both Mill and Malthus.[56] At the very outset, Ricardo expressed his doubts to Mill as to whether 'the Government and laws of one state of society' were well 'adapted for another state of society'.[57] This, Ricardo correctly noticed, was 'one of the great difficulties of the science'.[58] His doubts arose from an obvious consideration, namely that

> the people of England, who are governors, have an interest opposed to that of the people of India, who are the governed, in the same manner as the interest of a despotic sovereign is opposed to that of his people.[59]

Furthermore, since the British public's general apathy towards the administration of India was taken as given by Ricardo, he held that even the 'outside' check of public opinion at home was not likely to be 'very active and will therefore not much tend towards the correction of abuses'[60] in colonial administration. He was led, therefore, to wonder whether the 'salutory dread of insurrection' was all that remained to check 'misrule and oppression' in that

[56] These exchanges are discussed in the broader context of the economist's position on the colonies in Donald Winch's *Political Economy and the Colonies*, pp. 160–61.

[57] *Letter to Mill*, 18 December 1817, 7:22.

[58] Ibid., p. 229.

[59] Ibid., 30 December 1817, 7:239.

[60] Ibid.

country.[61] Ricardo, however, then proceeded to put his finger squarely on the problem with the new virtualism of Mill:

> Are we to fix our eyes steadily on the end, the happiness of the governed, and pursue it at the expense of those principles which all men are agreed in calling virtuous? If so might not . . . [any] . . . ruler, disregard all the engagements of his predecessors, and by force of arms compel the submission of all the native powers of India if he could show that there was a great probability of adding to the happiness of the people by the introduction of better instruments of government?[62]

The difficulty Ricardo foresaw, then, was precisely that problem which was at the core of any theory of virtual representation (and to which he had repeatedly objected to Trower). Furthermore, when the new virtualism arose out of the theory of utility, the problem took the form of having to determine 'how to balance one object of utility against another'.[63] In short, what Ricardo seems to have been raising here was the whole problem of interpersonal comparisons of utility (and this, a good forty years before the younger Mill came across it in the course of his elaboration of the harm principle in *On Liberty*). Unfortunately, no reply to these queries from Ricardo is extant.

But the correspondence between the two surrounding Mill's *History of British India* that we have just now been discussing also impinges directly on the question of representative government. In his very first letter, praising Mill's performance, the ever modest Ricardo declared that he was now 'anxiously disposed to understand'[64] the science of legislation, and that he entertained 'sanguine expectations' as to the 'practicability of improvements in legislation'.[65] To this Mill replied that he had no doubt that 'we shall now understand one another' on that subject, and he asserted that '[t]he ends are there, in the first place, known—they are clear and definite', and that it remained only 'to determine the choice

---

[61] Ibid., 6 January 1818, 7:241.

[62] Ibid., pp. 241–42.

[63] Ibid., p. 242.

[64] Ibid., 18 December 1817, 7:229.

[65] Ibid., p. 228. This, it would seem, was no mere intellectual curiosity; negotiations were already underway with Lord Portarlington for what was to become his seat in the House of Commons.

of means'.[66] In saying this, of course, Mill was no more than re-
peating the method he applied in legitimating representative government in England; it was the necessary means to the greatest
happiness. In India, for Mill at least, the means would be different. When Ricardo, for whom the whole subject also seemed to
admit of questions of principle (of ends not just means), politely
enquired of Mill as to what one should do when exclusive focus on
the ends led, as it did in the case of India, to the justification of an
imperial despotism, Mill was silent.

Mill's silence on this crucial question was nothing if not fortu-
nate. If his essay on *Government* is to be taken at its word, which
purports to show that *only* representative government (however
attenuated his old-man's franchise might have been) is sanctioned
by the principle of utility, then his idea that the government of
India could safely be entrusted to the members of the Imperial
Parliament at Westminster would seem to contradict his best-
known contribution to the science of government. If, on the other
hand, we seek to rescue him from contradiction by reminding ourselves that, in fact, the principle of utility sanctions only a government representative of those capable of knowing what is in their
own best interest, and acting upon it, and that in nations like India
this might be a very few (perhaps even only one), then we should
only have plunged him into a deeper quagmire. For in that case
the theory of representative government as a government of the
'Democracy or Community',[67] as it is styled in *Government*, would
be fatally compromised.[68] It was left to John Stuart Mill to deliver
the philosophic-radical theory of representative government from

[66] *Letter to Ricardo*, 27 December 1817, 7:234–35.

[67] *Government*, p. 16. It is worth noting that Mill wanted his readers to understand by this 'the majority'. Thus he writes that '[w]hen we say the few . . . it is
of no importance whether we mean a few hundreds, or a few thousands, or even
many thousands. . . . A numerous Aristocracy has never been found to be less
oppressive than an Aristocracy confined to a few' (p. 21). The same chord is struck
again by Mill in the *Fragment of Mackintosh*, especially pp. 291–92.

[68] Having said this, it should be noted that Ricardo seems to have seen this
particular matter (which concerns the logic of Mill's argument) rather differently.
On reading Mill's essay in the summer of 1820, Ricardo wrote that it was 'a consistent and clear development of your own views' (*Letter to Mill*, 27 July 1820,
8:211). Two years later he sent a copy to Trower, recommending it as 'an excellent article and well reasoned throughout' (*Letter to Trower*, 25 January 1822,
9:154).

this impasse. He freely abandoned the claim that the principle of utility sanctioned only equal representation (even at home), and without a second thought declared that the ignorance of savages rendered an enlightened imperial despotism far superior to a 'native despotism'.[69]

At another level, of course, the differences between James Mill and Ricardo appear to be indicative of the presence of a cleavage that runs far deeper than resolving either the problem of interpersonal comparisons of utility or the problems of the government of India. Lying at the very heart of their respective approaches to representative government are two divergent themes which, it might even be said, mark the boundary between an instrumental and a more substantive conception of democratic politics. This is rendered particularly clear when one considers Ricardo's view of the function of a reformed politics and the issue of co-optation versus incorporation.

[69] *Representative Government*, p. 409.

✤ CHAPTER FIVE ✤

Co-optation and Incorporation

WHEN MALTHUS WROTE TO RICARDO in the autumn of 1819 that he could 'hardly contemplate a more bloody revolution' than the one he confidently expected to take place if universal suffrage and annual parliaments 'were effected by the intimidation' of the mob,[1] he was not simply giving an airing to his old-fashioned Whig credentials; he was voicing the widespread feeling of alarm that seemed to permeate the consciousness of the British governing classes of the day. As far as these segments of the population were concerned, revolution was in the air.[2] Throughout the country, events between 1815 and 1819 only seemed to confirm those fears.

In this highly charged atmosphere the Tory government had pushed through Parliament the suspension of habeas corpus, using as its pretext the civil disturbances that followed the meetings at Spa Fields in London in 1816. Though most of the parliamentary Whigs expressed their misgivings as to the need for so drastic a measure,[3] the contribution of their often intemperate and dispar-

[1] *Letter to Ricardo*, 14 October 1819, 8:107. Donald Winch has suggested that, in retrospect, Malthus welcomed the passage of the 1832 Reform Bill. However, it is well to remember that in contrast to Ricardo, Malthus's position on the reform and extension of the franchise marked him as quintessentially a 'Country' Whig of the old stamp, calling upon 'the country gentlemen and the middle classes' to serve as the mediator between the claims of the government and the demands of the popular masses (see Winch, *Malthus*, pp. 49, 90).

[2] Even those who have sought to play down the value of the classical Marxist class-struggle interpretation of this unrest have still had to concede the ubiquity of this social-psychological alarm among the ruling classes. The employment of spies, the meetings of secret parliamentary committees, and the widespread use of troops to police the countryside, all testify to its presence, and can hardly be ignored. The following comment seems to provide a representative case: 'The Home Secretary smelled sedition and treason everywhere and spent sleepless nights over the bundles of papers which have loomed so large in the minds of historians of this period ever since' (White, *Waterloo to Peterloo*, p. 11; see also p. 47, but compare the qualification made at p. 92).

[3] Some appreciation of the nature of the case the Whigs made against suspension may be gained from Samuel Romilly's intervention during the third reading of the bill for suspension (28 February 1817). He 'urged the House to pause, and

100

aging public pronouncements to inculcating the sentiment behind the alarm was not lost on Francis Place, who wrote to Thomas Hodgskin that 'the Ministers found by far their best support for the vile measures they contemplated in the Whigs, who by their abuse of the people gave their encouragement to the Ministers to go much further than they themselves had contemplated'.[4] On 7 November 1817, Jeremiah Brandreth, William Turner, and Isaac Ludlum were hanged for their part in the Derbyshire Rising. Twenty-three of their co-conspirators were transported or imprisoned.[5] The final warnings came with the protests of the Blan-

---

not to suffer any judge or magistrate to take any man into custody without the order of his majesty's privy council, signed by six privy councillors' (*Hansard* 35:805). Indeed, the Whigs effectively transformed the whole debate on the third reading of the bill into one between alternative interpretations of the legal provisions of the existing constitution, with the Whigs maintaining that the Crown already possessed sufficient legal powers to suppress such 'violent proceedings' (as Lyttleton, who voted against, called them in the same debate; *Hansard* 35:798). Romilly's own account of his position on this subject can be found in his diary for February 1817 (in his *Memoirs* 3:276–80), where he records that he 'spoke on this, and, in the course of my speech, observed that, before we made new laws, it was necessary that we should know what had been done to enforce those which already exist' (3:277). In the House of Lords, Lord Holland's main concern was whether those detained would still retain the right to petition parliament.

[4] *Place to Hodgskin*, 30 May 1817, quoted in Graham Wallas, *The Life of Francis Place*, p. 123. Place actually singled out Henry Brougham for particular attack: 'Brougham came to England just before Parliament met, and finding himself disappointed for Westminster, knowing, too, that unless he made a strong party among the Whigs he would not be in the next Parliament, he at once took a most decided part against the petitioners for reform. Their petition was for annual parliaments, and pretty generally for universal suffrage. Brougham called them all manner of vile names, and imputed to them all manner of vile motives—they were ignorant, deluded, vile, mischievous incendiaries, &c. &c' (pp. 122–23). Here is how the radical Samuel Bamford summed up Brougham in his *Life of a Radical*: 'Oh! how he did scowl towards us—contemn and disparage our best actions and wound our dearest feelings! Now stealing near our hearts with words of wonderful power, flashing with bright wit and happy thought; anon like a reckless wizard changing pleasant sunbeams into clouds' (2:29). This kind of opinion of Brougham has to be understood in the context of what the Radicals seem to have seen as his earlier 'opportunism' in pledging his support for the whole Radical Reform platform in 1814 in an (abortive) attempt to be returned for Westminster (see the account of this episode in Francis Hawes, *Henry Brougham*, pp. 94–95).

[5] On this subject, see the account given by E. P. Thompson in *The Making of the English Working Class*, pp. 723–34 (who carefully discusses the role of the

keteers and, in August 1819, the massacre at Manchester (Peterloo), in consequence of which the Lords and the Commons rushed to pass the infamous Six Acts. These measures, too, entered the statute books on the back of large parliamentary majorities.[6] Even the more advanced Whig opinion-makers outside parliament, while their suggested remedies were different, were not immune to the alarm. Francis Jeffrey may be taken as only one example. In February 1817 (after Spa Fields) Jeffrey could still write 'as to plots and rebellions, I confess I am exceedingly sceptical'.[7] But, by 1819 (after Peterloo) his tone had changed markedly. 'We are not', he wrote then, 'in a good state in England, and I sometimes fear that tragical scenes may be before us'. In the absence of reform, and the continuation of repression, Jeffrey foresaw a 'sanguinary revolution'.[8]

Inside parliament, Henry Brougham's speech to the House of Commons on one of the Six Acts, the Seditious Meetings Prevention Bill (2 December 1819), seems to stand as exemplary of the Whig position. At Manchester there had been, Brougham fully conceded, an 'abuse of the right to petition',[9] and some of the speeches delivered there had been full of 'folly and wickedness'.[10] Brougham assured the House, however, that he did not think the banners containing the slogan 'Liberty or Death' were nearly as threatening as they had been made out to be. Even the banners calling for 'Equal Representation or Death', he remarked, were displayed in a spirit of 'mirth and good humour'.[11] What Brougham was against, and here he can safely be said to have been fully rep-

---

government *agent-provocateur* in the events leading up to the rising itself). Selections from the court's judgement are reprinted in Black's *British Politics*, pp. 19–25.

[6] The measure against which Ricardo spoke in the Commons debate, the Seditious Meetings Prevention Bill, for example, passed its third reading on a vote of 313 for, and 95 against (see Sraffa's editorial annotations in Ricardo's *Works and Correspondence* 5:29).

[7] *Letter to Charles Wilkes*, 17 February 1817, in Cockburn's *Life of Jeffrey* 2:166. Charles Wilkes, Jeffrey's father-in-law, was a banker in New York and the nephew of the famous John Wilkes.

[8] Ibid., p. 189.

[9] *Hansard* 41:664.

[10] Ibid., 41:665.

[11] Ibid. On the subject of the banners which were displayed at St. Peter's Fields, see the account given by R. J. White in *Waterloo to Peterloo* (p. 182).

resentative of Whig thinking as a whole, was the 'subversion of a great popular right': namely, the right of all subjects to petition. In short, in complete conformity with the sentiments of the movers of the Bill, Brougham wished to put a stop to Manchester-like 'irregularities'; but not at all costs. Whig philosophy held, quite simply, that an end to the revolutionary madness should be sought within the existing framework of legislation and without introducing new (repressive) measures that might actually work to subvert already existing constitutional rights.[12]

Given the turbulence of the times, exacerbated throughout the decade by increasingly repressive legislative responses (to which Ricardo was no less alert than any of his contemporaries), it seems prudent to focus rather more closely upon the impact of these events and attitudes on Ricardo's thinking about politics. The question one must ask is how far did they enter into, and colour, Ricardo's politics. Of particular interest in this regard is what Ricardo took to be the function of building a more inclusive political society. The received opinion, that he saw reform exclusively as 'the most efficacious preventative to revolution',[13] to use Ricardo's own words, would seem to suggest that for Ricardo political inclusion functioned as a means of social control; it was, so to speak, a buy-off, a device for co-opting dissenting opinion before matters got out of hand. However, the possibility that there might also have been something more substantive actuating Ricardo's politics should not be dismissed too quickly.

Exploring this possibility is not just a theoretical nicety or a matter of finding some comfortable ideological label with which to tag Ricardo. It helps to clarify how Ricardian politics might fit within a celebrated typology first applied systematically to the subject of political development by T. H. Marshall. In the course of his discussion of the movement towards democratization in the West,

---

[12] Given this kind of argument, it is hardly surprising that James Mill should have characterized the Whigs as the party of a 'perpetual system of compromise, a perpetual trimming' (from his article on the *Edinburgh Review* for the first number of the *Westminster Review* in 1824 and quoted in Nesbitt's *Benthamite Reviewing*, p. 40).

[13] *Letter to Mill*, 10 August 1819, 8:49. That reform might act to dampen revolutionary tendencies was something that even the Whigs like Francis Jeffrey had apparently come to believe by 1819 (see his *Letter to Charles Wilkes*, 24 August 1819, in Cockburn's *Life of Jeffrey* 2:189).

Marshall drew a distinction between two impulses which, according to him, were integral to its progress.[14] Broadly speaking, one of these had to do with the economic consequences of the rise of capitalism; the other was bound up with expanding conceptions of the nature of citizenship. The former advanced the cause of democracy in response to growing unrest consequent upon changing (usually worsening) social and economic conditions, while the latter advanced it consequent upon changing conceptions of the character of social and political rights. According to Marshall, democracy owed its advance in the West to a complex and subtle interplay between these instrumental and substantive tendencies.

The relevance of these ideas to an understanding of Ricardian politics may, perhaps, most readily be appreciated by considering for a moment the general tenor of a few other well-known economic theories of politics. For it appears to be the case that in many of them, the instrumental element in the argument is sometimes their most striking feature. Furthermore, this seems to hold good no matter which end of the political spectrum their respective authors might be thought to occupy. Thus, for example, among existing economic approaches to politics there is a very familiar one in which the basic theme seems to be that economics should lead and shape politics.

To take one recent example, many of Milton Friedman's arguments provide good illustrations of the leading role of economics over politics. Having posited the superiority of unregulated capitalist economic arrangements over all other forms of economic organization, Friedman argues that both the organization and the function of politics derive from the task of preserving the widest possible scope for capitalist activity. On this conception of politics, the character and function of representative government is dramatically narrowed. Friedman's vision of political action seems to be so completely subservient to his vision of the economy, that he readily claims that the unregulated market mechanism itself is seen as 'a system of effectively proportional representation',[15] one that surpasses in principle and practice anything that can be achieved through politics. This view renders claims for political reform (such as Ricardo's advocacy of widespread enfranchisement

[14] T. H. Marshall, 'Citizenship and social class' (1946).
[15] *Capitalism and Freedom*, p. 23.

and frequent parliaments) either beside the point, or even dangerous:

> The use of political channels . . . tends to strain the social cohesion essential for a stable society. . . . If it goes so far as to touch an issue on which men feel deeply yet differently, it may well disrupt the society. . . . The religious and civil wars of history are a bloody testament to this judgement. . . . The widespread use of the market reduces the strain on the social fabric by rendering conformity unnecessary with respect to any activities it encompasses.[16]

Friedman, of course, claims to draw support for this argument from the liberals of the early nineteenth century,[17] and in some sense his arguments have a distinctively utilitarian air reminiscent of certain of those thinkers. For example, Friedman appears to share James Mill's idea that unanimity is an ideal to be achieved within the community; and one which, in principle at least, politics could serve instrumentally to foster. And there is more than a trace of Bentham's dictum to the state, 'stand out of my sunshine', in much of what Friedman has to say. However, writing in the twentieth century, Friedman also realises that in politics diversity is the persistent reality, so that the use of politics to promote unanimity in practice requires coercion. This leads Friedman to reject the political sphere as the appropriate arena for securing precisely those ends (the greatest good) which the philosophical radicals had hoped to obtain from it, and to place instead all of his hopes on the market:

> The wider the range of activities that are covered by the market the fewer are the issues on which explicitly political decisions are required and hence on which it is necessary to achieve agreement. In turn, the fewer the issues on which agreement is necessary, the greater is the likelihood of getting agreement while maintaining a free society.[18]

Notwithstanding Friedman's own arguments to the contrary, however, once this step has been taken, any remaining commitment to representative democracy must be seen as purely instrumental.

[16] Ibid., pp. 23–24.
[17] Ibid., p. 5.
[18] Ibid., p. 24.

None of this, of course, should be taken as an attempt to deny the obvious; namely, that in the vast majority of cases there will always be both instrumental and substantive tendencies at work in the argument for democratic politics. Nor is it to claim that for certain purposes it would be anything other than artifice to separate them out. However, it does appear to be the case that something of the essential flavour of an argument may be overlooked if no attempt at all is made to distinguish between them, and to describe the consequences of each for the vision of politics at hand. The really interesting question, therefore, is how both of them might be said to have played out their respective parts in Ricardo's politics.

When one reflects upon the possibilities, there would seem to be a number of ways in which instrumental considerations might have coloured Ricardo's thinking about politics.

To begin with, they might have been introduced as a direct result of bringing to bear the conclusions of political economy in the advocacy of representative government. After all, Ricardo's economics had placed at the centre of the stage a conflict between well-defined economic interests: between landlords and capitalists on the one hand, and between capitalists and workers on the other. Armed with this kind of conflictual economic model, a democratic polity might have been conceived by him as a means of ameliorating endemic economic conflict. The advocacy of representative government would then have become, in form and substance, a self-conscious act of co-optation, offered as a *quid pro quo* for a greater degree of social stability.

Unfortunately, the difficulty of attributing this kind of argument to Ricardo is that while he never doubted that existing popular unrest was the necessary consequence of the presence of *unrepresented* rival economic interests in capitalist society, he never once thought that this underlying economic rivalry would simply vanish once the vote was granted. In fact, quite the reverse was the case. Even when (as Ricardo's economics very clearly revealed) those competing interests were not just those of different individuals, but were those of different social classes, Ricardo seems to have been perfectly comfortable with the idea that politics existed precisely to allow all those economic interests to gain political expression, rather than to quiet them. Ricardian politics, then, was not a politics of unanimity or harmonization, where there is a one-to-one mapping from political stability to economic harmony and back again. It was rather a politics which seems to have envisaged the possibility of a dynamic equilibrium, where the economic conflict inherent in market society only acted to pre-empt stability in the political nation when existing antagonistic class interests were un-equally represented.

Ricardo's position with respect to the land-owning classes, for example, seems to have been quite typical of this dimension of his thinking. The theory of differential rent, upon which that position was based, is unambiguous enough. The price of corn is deter-mined at the margin of cultivation, so that all intra-marginal land under cultivation commands a rent contingent upon 'the differ-ence in the quality' of that land relative to the quality of the 'less fertile' land at the margin.[19] Thus arises Ricardo's famous doctrine that rent is everywhere the *effect* of a high price of corn, and never the *cause*.[20] From this, in turn, derives the familiar argument that, as Ricardo put it in his *Essay on Profits*, 'the interest of the land-lord is always opposed to the interest of every other class in the community'[21] or, as it is stated in the *Principles*, their interests are 'always opposed to that of the consumer and the manufacturer'.[22]

[19] Ricardo seems to have taken the fertility of different types of land as given. Thus, he writes: 'If all land had the same properties, if it were unlimited in quan-tity, and uniform in quality, no charge could be made for its use, unless where it possessed peculiar advantages of situation. It is only, then, because land is not unlimited in quantity and uniform in quality, and because in the progress of pop-ulation, land of an inferior quality, or less advantageously situated, is called into cultivation, that rent is ever paid for the use of it. When in the progress of soci-ety, land of the second degree of fertility is taken into cultivation, rent immedi-ately commences on that of the first quality, and the amount of that rent will depend on the difference in the quality of these two portions of land' (*Principles* 1:70). He is speaking here, of course, of the extensive margin.

[20] *Principles*, 1:77. The argument was reiterated by Ricardo in his *Protection to Agriculture* in 1822: 'It is now universally admitted, that rent is the effect of the rise in the price of corn, and not the cause' (4:212).

[21] *Essay on Profits*, 4:21.

[22] *Principles*, 1:335. Elsewhere, Ricardo writes that it is on the basis of this the-ory that 'I have grounded my assertion that the interests of landlords are opposed to those of the other classes of society' (*Notes on Malthus* 2:198). This position was roundly attacked by Malthus who (quoting Smith) retorted that 'it seems scarcely possible to consider the interests of the landlord as separated from the general interests of society' (*Principles*, p. 194). Given the fact that these two economists had exactly the *same* theory of rent (Ricardo expressly acknowledged

However, as Ricardo was quick to record in his notes on Malthus's *Principles of Political Economy* in 1820, this did not mean that he 'considered them as enemies of the state'.[23] Rather, the problem was that these interests enjoyed a monopoly in political power; and this, courtesy of the existing state of representation.

So anxious does Ricardo seem to have become about clarifying the implications he wished to draw from the theory of rent, that he wrote a long passage attempting to distil his own position in a letter to Trower in July 1820. Its clarity is such as to render it worth quoting at length:

> [Malthus] represents me as holding the landlords up to reproach, because I have said that their interests are opposed to those of the rest of the community, and that the rise of their rents are at the expence of the gains of the other classes. The whole tenor of my book shows how I mean to apply those observations. I have said that the community would not benefit if the landlords gave up all their rent—such a sacrifice would not make corn cheaper, but would only benefit the farmers.—Does not this shew that I do not consider landlords as enemies of the public good?[24]

The problem was, of course, that on this front Ricardo was fighting against a reading of his work that was especially convenient both for his detractors (like Malthus) and his philosophic-radical friends alike.

Before the appearance of Ricardo's theory of rent in the *Essay on Profits* in 1815, the literature of political economy was already stamped with a relatively pronounced sentiment critical of the old landed aristocracy. In a certain sense, the science of political economy might even be said to have cast its lot against the landed interest as far back as the middle of the eighteenth century—at the very moment of its founding. It is clearly audible in the voice of Adam Smith when he speaks of the 'great proprietors'; although in

---

Malthus's primacy over him as to its origin), their dispute on this matter has more to do with their respective politics; with Malthus taking up the old-fashioned Whig cause.

[23] *Notes on Malthus* 2:117.

[24] *Letter to Trower*, 21 July 1820, 8:207–8. These remarks should, however, be supplemented by Ricardo's tirade against the Irish aristocracy in his *Letter to Trower*, 24 July 1823, 9:314. The latter question is discussed at length by R.D.C. Black in his *Economic Thought and the Irish Question*, p. 21 et seq.

his customary manner, it tended to gain expression in the form of caustic little asides about the wastefulness of expenditures devoted to the maintenance of large retinues of retainers,[25] or about the relatively backward state of agricultural production allowed to persist in certain aristocratic county seats (where stately homes often had their immediate environs decorated with ornamental gardens and parklands),[26] rather than in outright attacks on their place in the great chain of being. Arthur Young's well-known journals of his tours through the Kingdom, when describing similar scenes of agricultural backwardness, sometimes served to reinforce the opinion. Despite these reservations, of course, Adam Smith himself retained the more traditional view that the economic interests of the landed classes as a whole could never be in conflict with those of the nation.[27] But by the second decade of the nineteenth century, what might legitimately have been characterised as a murmuring of disquiet just fifty years before, had grown into a veritable chorus of abuse; especially in economic circles. In his widely used edition of the *Wealth of Nations* which appeared in 1814, David Buchanan, to take one example, had appended to the famous passage from the *Wealth of Nations* where Smith remarked that landlords 'love to reap where they never sowed',[28] an editorial note:

> They do so. But the question is why this apparently unreasonable demand is so generally complied with. Other men love also to reap

[25] See, for example, *Wealth of Nations*, 2.iii:332–34.

[26] Here is what Smith actually had to say: 'It seldom happens . . . that a great proprietor is a great improver. . . . The situation of such a person naturally disposes him to attend to ornament which pleases his fancy, than to profit for which he has so little occasion. The elegance of his dress, of his equipage, of his house, and household furniture, are objects which from his infancy he has been accustomed to have some anxiety about. The turn of mind which this habit naturally forms, follows him when he comes to think of the improvement of land. He embellishes perhaps four or five hundred acres in the neighbourhood of his house, at ten times the expence which the land is worth after all his improvements' (*Wealth of Nations*, 3.ii:385–86). It ought not to be forgotten that the eighteenth century was the great age of British landscaped gardens. Just two years before this was written, Lancelot 'Capability' Brown had completed his re-working of Sir John Vanbrugh's gardens at Blenheim Palace.

[27] *Wealth of Nations* 1.xi:265.

[28] Ibid., 1.vi:67.

where they never sowed, but the landlords alone, it would appear, succeed in so desirable an object.[29]

Furthermore, in the July number of the *Eclectic Review* for 1814, James Mill had spoken of a conflict of interest between landlords and the community as a whole, and had even warned them of the grave consequences of their continuing to exercise that interest once the majority of the people came to see more clearly its sinister character.[30] This strong statement from Mill came just ten years after his rather more circumspect remarks on the same subject in his *Essay on the Impolicy of a Bounty on the Exportation of Grain*.[31] That the view had spread well beyond the narrow confines of economic theorists by the turn of the nineteenth century can also hardly be doubted. Maria Edgeworth, it is well to remember, had actually made her literary reputation thanks to her portrayal of a dissolute aristocracy in *Castle Rackrent* (1800).

The pervasiveness of this kind of attitude towards the great proprietors probably helps to explain why it was Ricardo's name that came to be attached to the new theory of rent, rather than the names of either of its co-discoverers, Edward West or Malthus. For it was Ricardo's presentation, with its explicit juxtaposing of landed interests against the interests of the nation, that best matched the climate of the times in economics on the subject of old aristocracy. More so than West, who said almost nothing on the subject of the legitimacy or otherwise of the landed interest;

[29] The annotation is quoted by Edwin Cannan in his edition of the *Wealth of Nations* (Modern Library ed., 1965) in n.7 at p. 49.

[30] See the discussion of this argument in Halévy's *Philosophic Radicalism*, p. 278.

[31] That essay concluded with the following statement: '[N]either are the landlords to be blamed for making of their property as much as they can . . . [n]either can they be accused of generally besieging the legislature for laws, to favour their peculiar interests. . . . I am even persuaded were they once convinced that the late corn law is prejudicial to the interest of the country, that they would be the first to petition for its repeal' (p. 69). How far this kind of argument was a tactical decision on Mill's part, with the intention of playing down the attack in an effort to secure support for the measures he proposed, is difficult to tell. It is, however, worth noting that at the beginning of this essay he had said of the landlords' support for a higher price of corn that they 'liked this cry much better, . . . [t]hey joined in it; for their interest naturally prevented them from seeing its absurdity . . . [t]hey came to parliament for assistance to export corn, till the farmers could sell it high enough to pay them their present rents' (p. 4).

and certainly more so than Malthus, who actually stood against the tendency and staunchly defended the landed interest.

Whatever the lesson Ricardo himself drew from the theory of rent, it is quite apparent that it involved him neither in a programme for the euthenasia of the land-owning classes (of which he himself, it is well to recall, had become a member), nor one of land nationalization (nor, for that matter, in a campaign for a single tax). In an important sense, the message Ricardo took away from the theory of rent was more truly political than that. However radical some of the economic policies 'deduced' from Ricardo's theory of rent by subsequent generations of interpreters might have been, Ricardo seems to have chosen to turn the economics to the cause of representative government—that is, directly to the question of the constitution of political society itself.[32]

Some of Ricardo's own philosophic-radical friends, of course, were to give a rather different gloss to the Ricardian theory of rent. Since they had already staked out their opposition to the land-owning classes, Ricardo's new theory gave them (or so they thought) a more secure theoretical base from which to re-launch their old attacks. It was from that source, after all, that James Mill claimed to have discovered grounds sufficient for him to advocate the concentration of the ownership of land in the hands of the Crown in the case of British India.[33] He had also been led to support the taxation of landlords' income on essentially the same grounds.[34] John Stuart Mill (always anxious to distinguish between that part of landholders' income which derived from their investment in improvements on the land and that which derived exclu-

---

[32] This turn in Ricardo was noticed by Max Beer, who argued that in consequence of the theory of rent 'agitation for Parliamentary reform . . . appeared theoretically established and justified' (*History of British Socialism* 1:153).

[33] This, at least, is how the late Eric Stokes put it: '[T]o advocate an agricultural system based on relatively small peasant holdings was in itself sufficiently startling for a man of Mill's political leanings; but to advocate State ownership or nationalization of the soil was to strike at the whole Liberal tradition for which the institution of private property was the tap-root of progress and individual liberty' (*The English Utilitarians and India*, p. 87). In a broader context, it may be noticed that Francis Place was also a supporter of land nationalization throughout most of his life; having been converted to the idea by Thomas Spence in the late eighteenth century (see Wallas's *Life of Francis Place*, p. 61 et seq., and p. 173 & n.2).

[34] *Elements of Political Economy* 4.xi:284–85.

111

sively from their monopoly in its ownership), deployed the Ricardian theory of rent to champion a rent-charge for which 'the landlords are entitled to no compensation'.[35] A little later in the century, the whole single-tax movement under the charismatic leadership of Henry George would lay claim to being the heir of what, by then (in those circles at least), had become known as the Ricardian theory of the 'unearned increment'. While none of this is especially Ricardian, it does seem to provide another in that long line of instances in which it would be quite wrong to underestimate the potency of Ricardo's contribution to the course of practical politics.

Parallel to the conflict of interest between landlords and the rest (especially capitalists), ran a conflict of interest between capitalists and workers. In Ricardian economics, this conflict gained expression in Ricardo's celebrated theorem that there existed an inverse relation between the real wage rate (or the wage share) and the rate of profit. 'Profits, it cannot be too often repeated, depend upon wages', Ricardo emphasised in the *Principles*; to which he added the necessary clarification: 'not on nominal, but real wages'.[36] This conflict, too, was permanent and deeply embedded, so to speak, in the economic structure of society (or, more accurately, this is how it was viewed by Ricardo). Yet, as we have already noticed, this fact of economic life failed to shake Ricardo's confidence in the stability of a political order in which all class interests were given equal claim to be heard (and acted upon).

One might legitimately ask how far such a vision of political stability is consistent with Ricardo's well-known theory of subsistence wages. If, after all, the natural tendency of real wages is to settle at some minimum level in the long run, then one might expect the class whose living depended entirely upon wages to be constantly seeking to augment those wages with the assistance of their newfound political power. The problem, if it is thought of as such, would only be compounded if that class happened also to be the most numerous in civil society. This was the thought which accelerated John Stuart Mill's subsequent turn away from pure democracy (as he called it) on the grounds of its potential to facilitate

---

[35] Ibid., 5.ii:§6.
[36] *Principles*, 1:143.

working-class domination.[37] At the opposite end of the political spectrum, the same thought seems to have contributed towards boosting Marx's confidence in the real potential for a revolutionary transformation of capitalist society orchestrated by the proletariat for itself. The question to be faced is why Ricardo does not seem to have been led to one or the other of these two conclusions.

A remote possibility is that the thought just did not cross his mind. However, given that the whole of the political discourse which surrounded him at the time was ringing with voices reminding him of it, such an argument would seem to be difficult to sustain. The fact that Ricardo was not deaf to all of this is, perhaps, nowhere better illustrated than in one of his last parliamentary votes; that on the third reading of the bill for the repeal of the Spitalfields Acts (1773, 1792, and 1811) which took place on 11 June 1823. Ricardo had certainly heard the voice of the Spitalfields silk weavers, who wished to retain the special privileges with regard to wage determination that they had enjoyed under the act, and in the face of their opposition he had voted for its repeal in a bill introduced by the Tory liberal (and newly appointed President of the Board of Trade) William Huskisson.[38] The grounds for his opposition to the Spitalfields weavers was not anti-labour but, on the contrary, that these weavers constituted a labour 'aristocracy' who enjoyed their privileges at the expense of other weavers across the country.

A more plausible possibility is that Ricardo's optimism on the subject had rather more to do with the content of his theory of wages, and with his account of the movement of real wages over time. It is, therefore, to that theory that one must turn to find the grounds for his apparent confidence; and to get to the bottom of this matter, certain theoretical niceties of the Ricardian theory of wages have to be remembered.

The very first of these is a fundamental analytical distinction between, to use Ricardo's own words, the 'quantity of food, necessaries, and conveniences' that go to make up the wages of labour

---

[37] It had even led him, as early as 1839, to advocate a new motto for the Radical politician: 'Government *by means of* the middle for the working class' ('Reorganization of the reform party', p. 288; italics in original).

[38] On Huskisson's role, and the events surrounding this piece of legislation, see Alexander Brady's *William Huskisson and Liberal Reform*, pp. 95–98.

and 'the natural price of labour'.[39] This distinction, which is the hallmark of the writings of the classical economists (even if it was not always adhered to as strictly by all of their number as logic demanded), was set out by Ricardo in the second paragraph of the fifth chapter ('On Wages') of the *Principles*. In modern jargon, it involves the distinction between the commodity composition of the real wage on the one hand, and the value of the real wage on the other. These two conceptions of real wages are quite different, and a failure to distinguish between them has been responsible for the introduction of many unnecessary confusions into discussions of the Ricardian theory of wages.[40]

According to Ricardo, the quantity of wage goods required for 'labourers, one with another, to subsist and perpetuate their race, without either increase or diminution'[41] is, in any given society under any given set of historical circumstances, taken as datum. The real wage is determined by the social and institutional conventions which prevail, together with the level of economic development attained, in the relevant place and time. In adopting this course, Ricardo was no more than following in the footsteps of Adam Smith who had stressed that by necessaries one must understand 'not only the commodities which are indispensably necessary for the support of life, but whatever the custom of the country renders it indecent for creditable people, even of the lowest

[39] *Principles*, 1:93. Note that in the first and second editions of the *Principles* Ricardo had used the phrase 'the natural price of wages' instead. This seems to have the advantage of being more descriptive of the formal definition of the concept.

[40] Consider, for example, the discussion of Ricardo on wages in the second chapter of E. A. Wrigley's *People, Cities and Wealth* (p. 23 et seq.). There a blurring of the distinction appears to have led the author to equate the Malthusian and Ricardian arguments about the relation between wages and profits (and, therefore, about 'the secular prospects for real wages') on a point that they explicitly disagreed about. Some appreciation of the extent of this disagreement (and also of its relevance to Wrigley's claim that Ricardo and Malthus were as one on the question of the possibilities for secular rises in what he calls 'real income per head') may be gained by listening to what Ricardo actually had to say about it to James Mill: 'Malthus thinks it monstrous that I should say labour had fallen in value, when perhaps the quantity of necessaries allotted to the labourer may be really increased' (*Letter to Mill*, 28 December 1818, 7:378). A more detailed discussion of the analytical significance of this point can be found in De Vivo's *Ricardo and His Critics*, chap. 3.

[41] *Principles*, 1:93.

order, to be without'.[42] Ricardo made broadly the same point, although according to Marshall he failed to repeat it often enough.[43]

It is not to be understood that the natural price of labour, *estimated even in food and necessaries*, is absolutely fixed and constant. It varies at different times in the same country, and very materially differs in different countries. It essentially depends on the habits and customs of the people.[44]

On the other hand, the natural price of labour (or the *value* of these commodity wages) is determined by the relative prices of the commodities entering into the subsistence wage bundle. In the theoretical framework of *Principles*, where the relative prices of all reproducible commodities are determined by the relative quantities of labour required for their production, the natural price of labour is nothing other than the amount of labour embodied in the wage. It is the real wage rate understood in this sense (namely, as the natural price of labour), that Ricardo argues varies inversely with the rate of profit; not wages in terms of 'coats, hats, money, or corn'.[45] To be sure, this inverse relation codifies an immanent conflict of interest between workers and capitalists, but it does not seem to do so in a way which suggested that it was likely to break out into open political warfare.

To begin with, it does not entail the idea that commodity wages vary inversely with the rate of profit. Indeed, Ricardo himself gave a numerical illustration of this point in the very first chapter of the *Principles*, in which he considered a case where a technological improvement was introduced which allowed the same quantity of

---

[42] *Wealth of Nations*, 5.ii:869–70. In his familiar way, Smith supplements this statement with a few examples of the differences which prevailed as regards such conventionally determined 'necessaries' in England, France, and Scotland at the time.

[43] *Principles of Economics*, p. 421.

[44] *Principles*, 1:96–97; italics added. In support of this claim, Ricardo cites Robert Torrens' *Essay on the External Corn Trade*. See also *Principles* 1:159 and *Letter to Malthus*, 29 April 1823, 9:282–83, for further statements to the same effect.

[45] *Principles*, 1:50. It should be noted that under the labour theory of value, proportional wages (that is, the ratio of the value of the total wage bill to the value of production) and the value of the wage (the natural price of labour) are equivalent. In this case, the inverse relation can also be expressed as one between proportional wages (as defined) and the rate of profit.

labour to produce double the quantity of commodities, and showed that as long as workers and landlords in the new equilibrium received less than twice the amount of commodities they enjoyed before 'wages and rent had *fallen* and profits *risen*; though . . . the quantity paid to the labourer and the landlord would have *increased*'.[46] That is, while the inverse relation between the value of the wage and the rate of profit holds here, there is simultaneously a rise in commodity wages. Since the commodity composition of the wage has not a little to do with the standard of living enjoyed by the mass of the population, there would seem to have been no reason for Ricardo to have been overly concerned that capitalism might have a tendency to reduce the standard of living of workers to such miserable levels as to prompt them to social revolution. Indeed, considered from this perspective it would seem that in reaching different conclusions, subsequent writers as different as John Stuart Mill and Marx may well have mistakenly overestimated this tendency.[47]

Before leaving this subject, it is worth remembering that the commodity composition of the Ricardian subsistence wage was derived from mapping a given set of necessary requirements (for food, shelter, clothing, heating, and the like) onto the actual space of commodities currently being produced. Whether the existing technology of consumption mapped these requirements onto, say, sack-cloth, or linen, was not at issue. At different times and places, as Ricardo quite explicitly stated, different outcomes were to be expected. With the advance of technology and with the accumulation of capital one would certainly expect the commodity composition of the subsistence wage to change quite dramatically; and for the better.

As for Ricardo's worst-case scenario, where population was 'pressing against the means of subsistence',[48] thereby raising the cost of production of corn, things were not entirely as bleak as is sometimes suggested. There was always scope for a freer trade in

[46] *Principles*, 1:49–50, italics added. Ricardo and Malthus were continually at loggerheads over this point. Ricardo repeatedly made attempts to clarify the matter in *Notes on Malthus*, 2:249–50, 258–59, 278, 322–24.

[47] As did the Ricardian Socialists; on this point see the observations made by Max Beer in his *History of British Socialism* (1:199). The idea expressed is that the socialist reading was too 'statical'; Ricardo's was 'dynamical'.

[48] *Principles* 1:99.

corn,[49] for a measure of accumulation so long as the rate of profit had not fallen to zero, and perhaps even for a rational population policy.[50] Nor should it be forgotten that during the whole of the period leading up to the exhaustion of these avenues of prosperity, which might be considerable, Ricardo argued that workers would

[49] Just how powerful this particular engine of growth could be, was later vouchsafed by Marshall. He went so far as to attribute England's escape from some of the worst consequences of the pressure of population on the means of subsistence to 'the opening of England's ports, in 1846', thereby admitting the produce of 'the wheat-fields of the world' and underwriting continued material prosperity (*Principles of Economics*, p. 576).

[50] Whether this ever went beyond his support for a concerted campaign advocating voluntary restraint (what Malthus had called 'moral restraint') is difficult to say. Ricardo's position on artificial birth control was, to say the least, rather more reserved than some of the other radicals of his day. Francis Place, for example, had argued for the superiority of artificial over prudential checks to population, without detailing specific methods, in his *Illustrations and Proofs of the Principle of Population* (1822). Ricardo had received the manuscript of this book from Place in early September 1821, and had recommended it to his own publisher as a 'triumphant' reply to Godwin (*Letter to Murray*, 9 September 1821, 9:58). If, however, Ricardo's remarks to Malthus at the time can be taken as accurate, in the manuscript Place must have been a little more specific as to the methods available than he was to be in the book. Ricardo stated that in it 'Place speaks of one of Owen's preventatives' (*Letter to Malthus*, 10 September 1821, 9:62). Ricardo apparently subscribed to the opinion that Place's suggested method (the sea-sponge) was one thought to have been recommended by Robert Owen who, so the tale ran, had gone to France to discover safe and effective methods for artificially checking the growth of the population (see *Works and Correspondence* 8:71n.1). Owen himself much later published a denial of the whole story in the *Morning Chronicle* for 8 October 1827, after his name had been linked with the practice by both Place and Richard Carlile in 1825. How much faith one can place in Owen's disavowal is an open question (but see chapter 3 above, for a similar incident where, when his views were made public, Owen strenuously denied ever having held them). In this connection, it is perhaps also worth noting that the story that Owen was linked to the advocacy of the practice had been current years before anyone ever printed it. It was certainly about in 1819, when Trower jokingly mentioned it to Ricardo in connection with an impending addition to the Trower family (*Letter from Trower*, 8:71).

Taking a broad view of the whole subject, while it is true to say that Ricardo does not seem to have taken exception to Place's claim that artificial preventatives were to be favoured over moral restraint (and there are nine pages of comments on the Place manuscript, and three letters to Murray, Mill, and Malthus, in which he had the chance to do so), he did remark to Malthus that he had some 'doubt whether it is right even to mention it' (*Letter to Malthus*, 10 September 1821, 9:62). The contrast between Ricardo and both Francis Place and John Stu-

find it possible to maintain the market price of labour above its natural price. In this state of society, he observed, 'the condition of the labourer is flourishing and happy . . . he has it in his power to command a greater proportion of the necessaries and enjoyments of life'.[51] Indeed, had Ricardo not been so firmly convinced by Malthus's predictions of the future rate of population growth, and had he given only a little more weight to the possibility that agricultural production might yet have further productivity advances in front of it, one quite as far-reaching in its effects as that beginning to be worked in the manufacturing sector by 'improvements in machinery, by the better division and distribution of labour, and by the increasing skill, both in science and art, of the producers',[52] he might have been able to do more than 'wish' that 'in all countries the labouring class should have a taste for comforts and enjoyments, and they should be stimulated by all legal means to procure them'.[53]

Of course, whether Ricardo was mistaken not to have given rather more weight to class antagonism, and rather less to the abil-

---

art Mill is brought into sharp relief when one recalls the role of the last two mentioned in the events surrounding the distribution in London of the so-called 'diabolical handbills' on birth control in 1823 (see Himes: 'Mill, Owen and Neo-Malthusianism'). Here, of course, there is also a contrast with James Mill who (in print, at least) was also somewhat elliptical on the subject (see, for example, his remarks in the essay on *Colony* for the Supplement to the *Encyclopedia Britannica*, p. 261).

[51] *Principles*, 1:94. It should be added that in an influential book on Ricardo's theory of profits in 1960, G.S.L. Tucker suggested that an interpretation of the Ricardian theory of subsistence wages more suited to the case of a progressive economy might involve a consideration of 'the various levels of the commodity-wage, corresponding to different rates of accumulation' (*Progress and Profits*, p. 113). This would have the effect of admitting secular rises in the commodity wage to take place *without* the concomitant condition that the market price of labour *differed* from its natural price. There is a passage in Ricardo's chapter 'Taxes on Wages' (cited by Tucker at p. 114) that lends some weight to this view: 'Suppose the circumstances of the country to be such, that the lowest labourers are not only called upon to continue their race, but to increase it; their wages would have been regulated accordingly' (*Principles* 1:220).

[52] *Principles*, 1:94. The perplexing fact that Ricardo left all discussion of the effects of improvements in agricultural productivity from this source to the chapter 'On Profits' (1:120; but see also the discussion in the chapter 'On Rent' between pp. 79–84) may have partly contributed to the pessimistic vision that many have come away with from reading the chapter on wages alone.

[53] *Principles*, 1:100.

ity of political society to survive the economic contestations that lay behind it, is one thing. The point, however, is that he did not. Ricardo's politics, in this context at least, does not seem to be open to the charge of having been a strategy of co-optation. Representative government was not seen as a means of putting an end to class conflict. To be sure, this does seem to entail a certain optimism about the ability of market society to remain intact, and prosper, despite the inclusion of conflictual economic interests into the sphere of political life.[54]

The Ricardian vision of politics as an arena for structuring such conflict, for putting competing class interests on a more equal footing so to speak, seems to constitute the substantive democratic tendency in Ricardo's thought. Yet while it does not have as its primary objective the elimination of differences, there can be little doubt that it was also conceived by Ricardo as having the potentially beneficial side-effect of removing the more violent manifestations of that contestation from the streets. In this secondary effect, as it might be called, one does encounter an instrumental element in Ricardo's argument for representative government. For Ricardo did claim that an extension of the electoral franchise might act to forestall any practical possibility of social revolution; he set out the idea in a letter to Mill in 1819:

> Reform is the most efficacious preventative of Revolution, and may in my opinion at all times be safely conceded. The argument against reform now is that people ask for too much, and that a Revolution is really meant. Would they be better able to bring about a Revolution, if reform was conceded? . . . Reform may be granted too late, but it can never be given too soon.[55]

As we have already seen, Ricardo was confident that the rebellion in Ireland at the end of the eighteenth century might have been avoided by reform, and he re-iterated the more general elements of his opinion in both his parliamentary speech on the Seditious Meetings Prevention Bill in 1819[56] and his *Observations on Parlia-*

---

[54] This is an element of Ricardian politics to which we shall have reason to return in chapter 7 below.

[55] *Letter to Mill*, 10 August 1819, 8:49–50.

[56] *Speeches and Evidence*, 6 December 1819, 5:28–29.

mentary Reform.[57] As late as 1821, he was still writing to Mill to the effect that

> the only prospect we have of putting aside the struggle which they say has commenced between the rich and the other classes, is for the rich to yield what is justly due to the other classes.[58]

In view of the very clear and explicit recognition in this kind of argument of the immanence of class struggle in capitalist society, it is interesting to recall that from the very same kind of observation the young Karl Marx would later see in universal suffrage not a means of 'putting aside' the class struggle, but a weapon (unintentionally forged, so Marx thought, by the bourgeoisie for the purposes of their own destruction) with which to conduct the class war and to win a world-historical victory for the proletariat. 'Electoral reform', as Marx observed in his 1843 commentaries on Hegel's theory of the state, 'in the abstract political state is the equivalent to a demand for its dissolution'.[59] While this is not to say that Marx thought the 'dissolution' of the state would be the necessary outcome of universal suffrage in every actual political state (the lament at its outcome in France in 1852 in the *Eighteenth Brumaire of Louis Bonaparte*[60] signals that much), what is striking about the argument is that despite taking up effectively the same vantage point from which Marx looked out and saw the destruction of the existing economic order, Ricardo looked out and saw its preservation and progress. If one were to ask why this was so, the

[57] *Works and Correspondence*, 5:495, 497.

[58] *Letter to Mill*, 28 August 1821, 9:45.

[59] *Critique of Hegel's Doctrine of the State*, p. 191 (italics omitted). This philosophical discourse, naturally, is not the only place in which Marx saw universal suffrage in this hyper-radical way. On 25 August 1852 he published an article in the *New York Daily Tribune* which contained the following assessment of the political significance of the Chartist platform: 'The six points of the Charter . . . contain nothing but the demand of universal suffrage, and of the conditions without which universal suffrage would be illusory for the working class, such as the ballot, payment of members, annual general elections . . . universal suffrage is the equivalent of political power for the working class of England' (*Surveys from Exile*, p. 264).

[60] This is how Marx put it himself: 'Universal suffrage seems to have survived only for a moment, in order that with its own hand it may make its last will and testament before the eyes of all the world and declare in the name of the people itself: All that exists deserves to perish' (*Eighteenth Brumaire*, pp. 20–21).

answer would be that Ricardo believed that what the labouring classes actually wanted was neither to co-opt nor to be co-opted; but rather to have their interests recognized, valued, and addressed—to have their voice incorporated into the regularised political discourse of the nation.

Ricardo's political response to the social unrest which surrounded him seems to have differed quite markedly from the response of John Stuart Mill to similarly disturbed social conditions years later. It is true that both of them were certainly led to bolster an advocacy of representative government with appeals to its instrumental advantages as a palliative for civil unrest. However, they differed quite dramatically in the conclusions they drew from this recognition of the ameliorative potential of democratic constitutional reforms. Ricardo, for his part, was led to support rapid and extensive reforms of the electoral franchise. John Stuart Mill, on the other hand, opted instead for caution; and advocated gradual change through more limited reforms of the system of representation.

As a radical but not a revolutionary, Ricardo's thoughts about revolutionary political change were as clear as they were unequivocal; he was set against it. This sentiment is perfectly apparent in what we have already had to say concerning Ricardo's position on the question of political exclusion, where his minimum qualification, so to speak, was an attachment to the existing régime of private property. Moreover, in the context of his comments on James Mill's essay on *Liberty of the Press* (written in 1821) for the Supplement to the *Encyclopedia Britannica*, when Ricardo turned to Mill's argument that the press should be free to exhort the people towards 'general resistance of the government',[61] he remarked that he would 'hesitate in agreeing to it' because he feared that it might 'make the overturning of a government too easy'.[62] This, however, does not seem to have been because he thought the possibility to be imminent. Just after the massacre at Manchester in 1819, for example, Ricardo wrote to Trower that the 'radical reformers are very unfairly treated' in that they were all 'lumped together' as

[61] *Liberty of the Press*, p. 15.

[62] *Letter to Mill*, 14 October 1821, 9:102. It might be worth noting that despite conveying these reservations to Mill, Ricardo did not hesitate to recommend the essay to Trower as being 'very good' just three months later (see *Letter to Trower*, 25 January 1822, 9:154.)

revolutionaries 'without proof or even examination',[63] and to Malthus (just before those events) he observed that while 'there may be a few wicked persons who would be glad of a revolution' he was persuaded that 'this object must be confined to a very limited number' of individuals.[64]

The implications of this complex of ideas for a rational reconstruction of the underlying character of Ricardian politics appear to be quite profound; for these opinions seem at once to frame and define the boundaries of Ricardian political discourse at the decisive level of political tactics. What is more, they seem to delineate this tactical space in a way which re-affirms a feature of Ricardian politics that has already come to our attention in other contexts; namely the essentially modern framework of concepts underpinning it. The first thing that is evident from them is that for Ricardo at least the strategic game was not to be played using tactics expressly designed to exaggerate the fear of revolution—as some have suggested was the case with James Mill.[65] In fact, the very idea that such a tactic might frighten the ruling classes into reform fails to ring true. Alarm was being so effectively inculcated in the minds of the government by the actual course of events, that it is a little fanciful to think that it required a further boost from the pen of someone like Ricardo. Moreover, the feeling of alarm was quite evidently provoking political repression rather than reform; so much so, that a strategy designed to turn it to the advantage of the reformers would seem to be somewhat wanting in practical appeal.[66] Be that as it may, Ricardo worked instead to clear the tactical space entirely of the idea that revolution was imminent; because this was an idea he evidently regarded as having been the invention of the enemies of reform in the first place. Certainly it played into the hands of potentially reactionary forces within the

---

[63] *Letter to Trower*, 28 December 1819, 8:146.

[64] *Letter to Malthus*, 9 November 1819, 8:129. Interestingly, the letter continues: 'neither do I observe in the speeches which are addressed to the mob any such extravagant expectations held out to them. If there were I am sure they know better than to believe the speakers who make such delusive promises' (8:130).

[65] Joseph Hamburger originated this argument in *James Mill and the Art of Revolution*.

[66] Then again, with James Mill almost anything could be made to look 'logical'. There is a further discussion of this aspect of Mill's thinking in the following chapter.

government (such as the more senior ministers of Lord Liverpool's cabinet[67]), and the opponents of reform within the country (such as Trower).

One of the interesting sidelights of all of this is the absence from Ricardo's thinking of any apparent sign or remnant of the old eighteenth-century notion that rebellion (or, at least, the threat of it) constituted one of those ancient rights enjoyed by the freeborn Englishman which secured his liberty against a local tyranny. Of course, it is not that Ricardo supported the limitation of public discussion. Ricardo's advanced position on the freedom of the press and on the freedom of religious belief testify well enough to that. It is rather that the grounds upon which such liberties existed were being couched by Ricardo in the modern, rather than in the old-fashioned way. The press, the pulpit, and the public parks and thoroughfares were regarded by Ricardo not as the locus of rebellion, but as the space in which opinions were expressed and formed, opinions which the people would subsequently look to their parliamentary candidates to address and, if elected, to promote within the legislature.

In the final analysis, of course, however subtle the turns of the argument, and however austere the form and outline of the theoretical apparatus, in matters of politics it is the principle that counts. The spirit which infuses the argument with its meaning and appeal, which brings it to life so to speak, is ultimately what gives to a political argument its most characteristic flavour. In the case of Ricardo, then, how might one summarise the essential spirit of Ricardo's politics? Probably in no better way than by allowing Ricardo to speak for himself. At the Anniversary Dinner of the Electors of Westminster on 23 May 1823 in the Crown and Anchor tavern, Ricardo rose to propose a toast; his words were to be the last that he would utter in public on the subject of citizenship.[68] They were reported in the *Morning Chronicle* the following day, and worth quoting:

[67] Nor should it be forgotten that it was not only Lord Eldon and Viscounts Sidmouth and Castlereagh, who were so inclined. Even Canning, with his established 'Anti-Jacobin' credentials, could be counted on to see sedition afoot and to join in its suppression. On this point, see, for example, the account in Dixon, *George Canning*, pp. 190–92.

[68] For Ricardo's last private word, see the passage from his *Letter to Mill*, 30

The only remedy for the national grievances, a full, fair, free, and equal representation of the people in the Commons' House of Parliament.[69]

But, of course, even Ricardo recognized that this was not enough. For after the composition of the reformed parliament had been determined, the important question of the frequency of elections had yet to be addressed. It is to Ricardo's answer to this question which we now turn.

August 1823, quoted at the end of chapter 7 below (*Works and Correspondence* 9:375).

[69] *Speeches and Evidence*, 23 May 1823, 5:484.

The Duration of Parliaments

THE SUBJECT of the frequency of elections was intensely debated both within the larger camp of moderate reform with which Ricardo associated in parliament between 1819 and 1823, and within that more intimate coterie of radical reformers with whom he was associated outside of it. For very nearly a century, the opponents of more frequent parliaments had argued that 'more frequent elections would encourage faction, sedition, and insurrection, and would disturb the balance of the constitution by increasing the influence of the electorate over their representatives'.[1] At issue for advocates (as well as opponents) of reform was the question of whether the greater populace, in whose name the adjustments in the franchise and the secret ballot were being demanded, required greater moral or technical education before their admission to the political nation could be safely secured. The answer which advocates of reform gave to this question determined in large part whether their writings conveyed a practical or purely hypothetical undertaking. In the case of the writings of the philosophical radicals like Bentham and James Mill, the demands of theoretical system and practical reform sometimes rested in uneasy tension. Of course, others outside the immediate circle of Ricardo's confidence characterized such reforms as more unnecessary in principle than dangerous. In this vein, one James Brown, a correspondent from Newcastle-upon-Tyne, wrote to Ricardo of his fears for a population incited by that 'mischievous Quack' Henry Hunt, 'who tells them of Annual Parliaments, Universal suffrage and Election by ballot being infallible nostrums for all their evils'. Rather than political reform, Brown had argued, 'the people want employment and nothing else'.[2]

Ricardo disagreed. His position on the 'necessity of more fre-

---

[1] H. T. Dickinson, *Liberty and Property*, p. 157. Robert Walpole had used just this argument in Parliament in 1734 in opposing a motion for the repeal of the Septennial Act (1716).

[2] *Letter from Brown*, 29 September 1819, 8:99.

quent elections' was perhaps the most crucial component of a thorough-going reform of parliamentary representation. It was based on the conviction that the need for representatives to recur more frequently to the electorate was neither a sop to the revolutionary tenor of popular opinion, nor an effort at co-opting such disgruntlement, nor yet an unrealistic and visionary scheme.[3] Rather, shortening the duration of parliaments was, for Ricardo, an effective democratic tool for recasting the function of political representation in parliament.[4]

The demand for more frequent elections complemented and completed Ricardo's proposals for the democratic reform of representation which had begun with an expanded franchise and the secret ballot. If secured, the two latter reforms would recast the character of the political nation both by enlarging the number and the diversity of interests and opinions routinely brought into parliamentary discussion and by ensuring the true expression of these interests at the point of election. As with his argument for the expanded franchise and the ballot, Ricardo's support for more frequent elections also depended crucially upon the case to be made for the value of the opinions and interests of the people in shaping

[3] *Letter to Malthus*, 9 November 1819, 8:129. Ricardo wrote to Malthus that his 'scheme of reform . . . is as much too moderate, as the universal suffrage plan is too violent,—something between these would give me satisfaction'.

[4] The issue of the frequency of parliaments had, of course, long and distinguished credentials in English political history. It was the slogan of the 'outs' against the 'ins'. Very early on, the cry for annuality was, as Betty Kemp observed, 'often supported by an appeal to "the statutes made in the reign of Edward III"', that is, the statutes of 1330 and 1362' which countenanced yearly parliaments for the redress of grievances (see *King and Commons*, p. 16). After the settlement of 1689, parliament acted to pass the Triennial Act (1694), mandating that 'a parliament shall be holden once in three years at the least' (see Adams and Stephens: *Select Documents*, p. 471), to back up its constitutional check on the power of the Crown. Not surprisingly, as soon as the Lords Spiritual and Temporal, and the Commons, felt rather more secure from encroachments on their own power from that source, they acted to pass the Septennial Act which fixed the duration of parliament at a maximum of seven years. Familiar reasons were advanced for this extension of the life of the parliament: experience, expence of election, and the disruptive effects of frequent election campaigns. The veracity of these claims need not detain us here. What is relevant, however, is the fact that in their claims for more frequent elections, the radicals of the early nineteenth century were, in a sense, merely echoing the demands parliament had been making for *its* authority over the Crown a hundred years before. This time, of course, the people were demanding a means to exercise *their* authority over parliament.

the course of parliamentary decision-making. It had to be shown that the voice of the people was worth listening to—and regularly at that. Ricardo's argument on this point may be contrasted with that of other philosophical radicals in his conviction that this voice could safely be listened to there and then, rather than after some future development of its moral character and intellectual tenor.

For example, in Ricardo's argument, unlike that of James Mill, the problem of representation does not appear to have been the lack of intellect or virtue among, in particular, the labouring classes. Ricardo neither wrote nor spoke in Mill's theoretical terms of the need to build a unified (and effectively middle class) 'community of interest' as the political foundation of representative government. As we have already seen, their views of the representative and his relationship to the constituent body differed. Having read the essay on *Government*, Ricardo wrote to Mill praising its 'true philosophic temper' and its 'clear and convincing' style. Yet Ricardo was not without reservations: 'I dare say you had good reasons for not explaining the influence of public opinion on government, but as it is one of the checks, and a most powerful one in such a government as ours, I should have expected that you would have noticed it'.[5]

Ricardo's reservations, however, were not entirely justified. Mill *had* discussed the role of opinion in the essay on *Government*. But it seems clear that the function Mill perceived for the public's voice in more frequently shaping government policy differed significantly from that of Ricardo. For Mill, the role of the people, and of public opinion remained one of opposition to government.[6] Indeed, Mill claimed in the 1818 essay that the greatest safeguard of the 'goodness of government' was to be secured by protecting the people's right to censure it.[7] As late as 1831, Mill suggested that to ensure reform the people 'should appear to be ready and

[5] *Letter to Mill*, 27 July 1820, 8:211.

[6] The idea of outside agitation in the form of public petitions, free press, and popular protest meetings was sometimes referred to by reformers as the use of 'steam' (as in letting off steam); see Joseph Hamburger, *The Art of Revolution*, p. 3. The focus of early reformers appeared to be on mobilizing extra-parliamentary protest by unenfranchised citizens. Hamburger claims that in this tactic the radicals borrowed heavily from the eighteenth-century constitution to frame their defence of extra-parliamentary agitation and so inevitably spoke in the language of constitutional rights to a free press and to public meetings.

[7] *Government*, p. 18. The essay contained a section on 'Of Exhortations to obstruct the Operations of Government, in detail' (pp. 16–17).

impatient to break out into outrage *without actually breaking out*.[8] Such statements may have been in large part responsible for the retrospective characterization of the philosophical radicals as at best pragmatic democrats—favouring reform as a preventative to revolution. The continued willingness to use the labouring class as a threat, and of envisaging the principle political role for the people as one exercised outside of government, poised and ready to check the sinister interest of 'their Rulers',[9] led Bentham to characterize Mill's democratical commitments as equivocal.[10] Whether Bentham's assessment is accurate or not, Mill's characterization of the actual political function of even an expanded electorate remained reminiscent of an eighteenth-century vision of popular protest which adjustments to its frequency of utterance would do nothing substantially to alter.

Understood in this way, it is hardly surprising to find that Mill made no direct argument for either annual or triennial parliaments in the essay on *Government*. On that subject, the essay in fact contains only one rather oblique and cryptic remark: namely, that the 'smaller period of time during which any man retains his capacity of Representative, as compared with the time in which he is simply a member of the community, the more difficult it will be to compensate the sacrifice of the interests of the longer period, by the profits of mis-government during the shorter'.[11] But Mill was quick to add that limiting the duration of parliaments should not work against the power to 're-elect the man who has done his duty'. He also recognized the benefit of re-electing the experienced representative, 'because the longer he serves, the better acquainted he becomes with the business of government'.[12] As discussed in chapter 2, Mill continued to place faith in the secret ballot, even as late as 1830, as the element of reform most needed to secure good government.[13] Indeed, some interpreters have

[8] Joseph Hamburger, *Art of Revolution*, p. 115.

[9] *Government*, p. 19.

[10] 'He argues against oppression less because he loves the oppressed many, than because he hates the oppressing few. He fights for the people—[not] that he cares for the suffering people, but that he cannot tolerate the suffering-creating rulers'. Bowring's editorial annotations to the correspondence with James Mill, in *Works* 10:432.

[11] *Government*, p. 18.

[12] Ibid., p. 20.

[13] 'The ballot', p. 1.

gone so far as to claim that the utilitarians 'put all their eggs in one basket'—and perhaps the wrong basket at that—namely, the secret ballot.[14] On the theoretical level this is not surprising, since the secret ballot goes well with the fear of corrupted interests so strongly expressed in all of Mill's political writings. Without electors whose choices can be made independently there could be no checking of the influence of 'sinister interest' in the constitution.[15] Secrecy, Mill believed, would ensure such independence.

Ricardo, however, did not view the role of public opinion in Mill's oppositional sense, and popular protest was never, for him, the best check on government. Nor did he see the need to educate an expanded electorate in how to choose representatives who would personify the virtue and interest of the community.[16] The problem of representation was not the labourer's lack of intellectual capacity (the masses had enough to function politically) nor virtue per se. In any case, for Ricardo these were not the appropriate building blocks of representation. What was needed was an adequate and frequent recurrence to the interests and desires— real and material rather than ideal and unified—of the people. Public opinion had, in some genuine sense, to be brought *into* government. This could only be accomplished with a reformed House of Commons and a more frequent recurrence to the electorate. Together these reforms could produce 'good government' in Ricardo's distinctive sense of that term.[17] Indeed, Ricardo argued that even the existing representatives themselves could be made to serve adequately the interests of this expanded electorate if only they were more frequently returned to office. Ricardo had no doubt that 'the aggregate of the House of Commons contained as much intellectual ability and moral integrity as ever existed in any similar assembly in the whole world'. 'But then', he noted, 'it must be recollected, that all men, in all situations, acted under the

[14] See William Thomas, 'James Mill's politics: the "Essay on Government" and the movement for reform', p. 284; see also Wendell Robert Carr, 'James Mill's politics reconsidered: parliamentary reform and the triumph of truth', pp. 553–80.

[15] Halévy, *History of the English People*, 1:12 (see especially the discussion of corruption, at pp. 8–10)

[16] This does not mean that Ricardo either ignored or opposed the need for education to be extended to the labouring classes.

[17] Ricardo, *Parliamentary Reform* 5:499.

influence of motives. He was persuaded that the conduct of the very same gentlemen by whom he was then surrounded, if they were really chosen by the people, and were frequently returned to the people that their merits might be re-considered, would be extremely different from that which it was at present'.[18]

The requirement of more frequent elections was thought by Ricardo to be 'indisputable', because it was the most 'ready means of insuring the attention of the House uniformly to the interests of the people'.[19] Ricardo was at pains to dispel, through the use of more frequent parliaments, any suggestion that individuals held 'vested rights' tantamount to property in the boroughs they represented—rights for which they might demand compensation in the event of parliamentary reform:

> Had not the people a right to be well governed? And was it to be maintained, that, because a certain set of persons had, for corrupt purposes, enjoyed the privilege for many years of preventing the people from being well governed, they should, therefore, be compensated for the loss of a privilege so unjustifiable?[20]

This view of representation seems to have been the most direct of any of the radicals save Bentham. Indeed, if we are to take seriously many of the subsequent commentaries on Bentham's political thought, it may have outstripped even 'the great subversive'[21] himself in its commitment to a more genuinely democratic politics.

In Bentham's account, the need for good government was to be achieved by the maximization of three elements in parliament under the heading 'appropriate aptitude'. These elements, appropriate probity, appropriate intellectual aptitude, and appropriate active talent, were juxtaposed to the three elements of the aristocratic or landed qualification: 'Blood, Property, Connexion'.[22] On this vision, the purpose of more frequent elections was to constrain the behaviour of parliamentary representatives, since Ben-

---

[18] Ibid., p. 288.
[19] Ibid., p. 285.
[20] Ibid.
[21] Bentham is characterized in these terms by John Stuart Mill ('Bentham', p. 79). James Mackintosh preferred to think of him as 'a hermit in the greatest of cities' (*Progress of Ethical Philosophy*, p. 190).
[22] Bentham, *Plan of Parliamentary Reform* 3:468–69.

tham believed (as did Ricardo) that an extended, even universal, suffrage alone would not do away with the 'influence of *aristocracy*' in politics.[23] '[M]y own persuasion is', wrote Bentham, 'that under the most unbounded universality of suffrage,—instead of being annihilated, the influence of the *aristocracy* would still be but too great: too great, I mean, with relation to appropriate *intellectual aptitude*: too great not to give admission to many an idle and comparatively unfurnished, to the exclusion of a laborious and better furnished, mind'.[24]

Both Bentham and Ricardo were, therefore, concerned with the inordinate and unjustified weight of influence exercised in parliament by an aristocratic interest and mentality. Both believed such interests were firmly entrenched under the existing septennial system, and on Bentham's account at least, such an entrenchment was not removable even by trienniality:

Under trienniality, *three years* is the term for which every man may sell himself to anybody . . . three years, the time given to him to remain in a complete state of *independence* as towards *constituents*; then in a state of complete *dependence* and mischievous obsequiousness, as at present, as towards his *purchaser*. Trampling on his duty—doing the work of political uncleanness with greediness, during the whole of the two first years, with a part more or less considerable of the last,—just at the close of the term—(adequate active talent being supposed to be in his possession)—by some dashing and momentary display of the exercise of the art of popularity-hunting, the corruption-hunter may have promised himself . . . the satisfaction of thus atoning for his past misconduct, in the eyes of a never-with-sufficient-universality-or-constancy-attentive, and for ever too indulgent, people'.[25]

On this reasoning, Bentham was led to favour annual elections. If what was needed in politics was more 'appropriate *intellectual aptitude* and *active talent*', then, he argued, annual elections ensured the 'promptitude of the remedy *maximized*'.[26] He also challenged the notion that annual elections would produce greater disruption and turmoil in the electoral process. On the contrary, he

[23] Ibid., p. 468n.
[24] Ibid.
[25] Ibid., p. 522.
[26] Ibid.

claimed that trienniality was more disruptive since it meant that 'the longer the term in the seat, the greater the value of the seat; the greater the value of the seat, the stronger the incitement in both situations,—that of the candidate and that of the elector; the stronger the excitement, the greater the temptation to disorder in every shape'.[27]

Bentham's proposals for electoral reform, including the expansion of the franchise, the use of secret ballot and frequent (preferably annual) elections, have been characterized by more than one of his interpreters as utilitarian positions developed in order 'to avoid, or to reduce to the smallest possible extent, the inconveniences involved in *elections*'.[28] On Halévy's understanding, to take just one well-known example, Bentham's political concerns were more technical than substantive; his aim was with the greatest simplicity of political procedure. For instance, Halévy suggested that Bentham's support for the secret ballot, with its attendant possibility of voting by mail, was preferred because it 'would do away with the tumultuous nature of the elections, and would simplify the examination of their validity'.[29] In the case of another proposed reform, Halévy argues that Bentham favoured the 'regularization of the right to vote' (that is, annual elections) both as a simplification of the task of the judges and as an added advantage in developing the 'appropriate intellectual aptitude' in the electors. In this sense, Halévy maintains, '[t]he reform has no direct advantages in its democratic aspect; strictly speaking, even, the regularization of the right to vote does not imply its democratization'.[30] Halévy's conclusion is thus that Bentham's practical political reform positions were significantly less a product of any intrinsically democratic political thought that he might have intentionally embraced than the necessary consequences derivative of his strict application of the utilitarian theory of action.

The attacks on Bentham by his contemporary critics among the Whig reformers, especially those of James Mackintosh, appear to support Halévy's skepticism as to the actual reform intentions contained in Bentham's arguments for annual parliaments. Mackintosh's own opposition to increased frequency of elections, for ex-

[27] Ibid., p. 524.
[28] Elie Halévy, *Philosophic Radicalism*, p. 258.
[29] Ibid., p. 259.
[30] Ibid.

ample, was precisely the opposite of the Walpolean fears of insurrection. Rather, Mackintosh claimed that they 'may be too frequent for exciting universal attention and national sympathy. Whatever is very frequent becomes familiar. It is viewed with little interest and no spirit.'[31] This, according to Mackintosh, was precisely the point of an unpublished *critique* of annuality by Bentham which he [Mackintosh] had 'the good fortune to possess', and which Mackintosh made public in support of his own opposition to annual parliaments in his celebrated article on universal suffrage for the *Edinburgh Review* for 1818. Bentham's arguments, as reported by Mackintosh, make clear that annuality was not the key to parliamentary reform:

> Next to the having no periodical elections, is the having them as frequent as possible. Why? Because, the oftener they come round the less danger there is of a change. As the mischiefs of changing so often as you might change are so palpable, and as you see no more reason for changing one time than another, you even take things as they are, and enter into a sort of implicit engagement with yourself not to change at all.
>
> This is no speculative conjecture: it is but a key to facts offered by experience. In England, wherever regular accession is not the object, (Examples: Lord Mayor of London: Sheriffs of London) annual elections prove in effect appointments for life, subject only to a periodical power of motion which is rarely exercised (Examples: Chamberlain of London: Chairman of the Justices of the Peace of Middlesex: President of the Royal Society—to which may be added, the Common Council of London) while longer terms produce frequent changes, and still more frequent struggles (Examples: Member of Parliament).[32]

Finally, more recent commentators on Bentham have to a large extent supported Halévy's rather negative evaluation of Bentham's contribution to modern democratic thinking. In particular, one of them has noted Bentham's admission that his preference for annual parliaments as well as universal suffrage (the more radical, rather than the moderate, proposals for reform) rested on their

---

[31] 'Universal suffrage', p. 198.

[32] Mackintosh, 'Universal suffrage', p. 199. The passage from which these remarks from Bentham are taken is cited by Mackintosh as being 'Remarks on the Judicial Establishments of France' (chap. 5, title 3).

greater congruence with the principle of utility than any deviation from them would be.[33] Bentham wrote that in the conflict between annuality and trienniality, utility mandated that annuality first was to be preferred:

> In the event of misconduct, the remedy is by a better choice. In the case of annuality, behold here promptitude maximized; in the case of trienniality, degree of promptitude no more than one-third of what it is in the other case.[34]

Likewise, in the case of improving *intellectual aptitude* and *active talent* in the form of either 'absolute or comparative' deficiencies among the electorate, annuality increased ('*maximized*') by two-thirds the '*promptitude*' of the triennial remedy.[35] The conclusion drawn from this line of interpretation is that it is unclear 'whether or when' Bentham ever became an intentional or 'committed democrat', since his arguments for key planks of the democratic platform (such as annuality) remained 'either speculative deductions from utility or preferences based on the estimate that popular elections appeared to be the least objectionable method of choosing governors'.[36]

Clearly, whether his principal aim was to do so or not, Bentham's writings forged a relationship between democratic principles and utility, but it was a relationship (like Mill's) which was distinctively negative in character.[37] Like James Mill, Bentham's

---

[33] Rosenblum, *Bentham's Theory of the Modern State*, p. 84. See also the *Plan of Parliamentary Reform* 3:599. James Steintrager, in a chapter from his *Bentham* entitled 'The Making of a Democrat', argues that 'although, as has been shown, there were potentially democratic elements in Bentham's formulation of the principle of utility, such as the psychological axiom that each one is the best judge of his own interest and the inclusion of equality as one of the four subsidiary ends, nevertheless by his own insistence he did not give any prolonged attention to constitutional questions nor become a democrat until 1809' (p. 78).

[34] *Plan of Parliamentary Reform* 3:521.

[35] Ibid., p. 522. In 'Universal suffrage' Mackintosh observed that even Bentham 'admits a principle of exception to universality of suffrage' based on a lack of 'appropriate intellectual aptitude' and/or on the grounds of illiteracy. Mackintosh also claimed that Bentham 'hesitated' over the admission of female electors, though not for reasons of incapacity or want of 'sense of virtue', but for reasons of utility—domestic peace and 'for the sake of the duties of their sex' (p. 192).

[36] *Bentham's Theory of the State*, p. 85.

[37] Ibid. Rosenblum argues that for Bentham 'the import of democratic representation was doubly negative, negative in both its object and the means to it'.

hatred of the corruptive proclivities of the aristocracy and of the King's ministers was almost unbounded.[38] On occasions he endorsed Mill's suggestion of using the threat of violence by the people-at-large as a tool of reform. On the whole, however, he reserved that hyperbolic role for intellectuals such as himself, whose writings aimed 'to strike and to shock the imagination of the public and make them dissatisfied with existing institutions' and to establish the necessary psychological preconditions of 'general abhorance' which Bentham felt must precede any effectual reform be it in law or politics.[39] To this end, Bentham seems to have willingly and willfully exaggerated his political demands. He gave little thought as to whether, as a practical matter, annual parliaments actually could be expected to function successfully to legislate the greatest happiness, or whether such frequency of election might disrupt the ability of any body of elected representatives to maintain a consistent line of policy in political or economic affairs. Of course, it is easy to see a way in which Bentham could have escaped this dilemma—by consigning, as he did, the domain of policy-making in these areas to technical experts (like himself) and to bureaucrats. In that way, annuality might be easily justified on the grounds that one expected politicians largely to do nothing—for either good or ill.[40] The difficulty with this, however, is that once again it would seem to compromise any genuinely democratic impulse behind elections. On this point, the comparison with Ricardo is particularly striking.

Ricardo was not the man of system when it came to politics. In particular, he did not share Bentham's desire for simplicity or 'niceness' when it came either to the arguments for, or the design of, institutional arrangements for political reform. Instead, Ricardo required that any proposal for constitutional revision (from the ex-

[38] On the issue of the participation of the labouring classes in electoral politics, Bentham confronted directly the issue which Ricardo chose (perhaps through delicacy) to avoid; namely, the old epithet of 'scum', as applied to the 'inferior class' of the people at large. Bentham simply re-applied it to the aristocracy: 'for be it a pot or be it kingdom, that which occupies the top of it, is it not the scum?' (*Constitutional Code* 9:57).

[39] *Philosophic Radicalism*, p. 305.

[40] This would certainly conform with the passages produced by Mackintosh to the effect that Bentham at one time actually opposed annuality on the grounds that it would tend to promote no changes whatsoever.

135

panded franchise to the increased frequency of elections) would make greater democratic participation congruent with stability in the development of governmental policy. On these grounds, Ricardo opposed annuality and settled on trienniality as his favoured reform proposal.[41] For Ricardo, trienniality struck the appropriate balance (the only notion of balance he thought important to representative government) between the need for more frequent recurrence to the people on the one hand, and the necessary degree of stability in government decision-making on the other. Moreover, it also supported what he thought was the need for a stronger and more direct link between the representative in parliament and those whom he was supposed to represent. Through the combined reforms of the franchise and the duration of parliaments that Ricardo maintained an 'intimate union between representatives and their constituents' could be forged.[42]

The adjustment of the relationship between the representative and his constituent to one of a more 'intimate union' is perhaps the most interesting and provocative aspect of Ricardo's proposed parliamentary reforms—and it is tied directly to his position on the need for the greater frequency of elections. More moderate Whig reformers, and here Francis Jeffrey furnishes a good example, had consistently argued that 'the true way then to silence the cry for annual parliaments, is *for septennial parliaments to do their duty*', just as he had argued that 'the grand antidote against the rage for universal suffrage, is for those who have been elected by a limited class of constituents, to act as if they considered themselves charged equally with the interests af all'.[43] As we have already indicated, one key to Ricardo's radical departure from moderate Whig reformers like Jeffrey rested precisely in his disagreement with their attachments to this older, and for Ricardo, empirically discredited, vision of parliamentarianism—a vision which construed the representatives' role as one of the 'independent' or 'private' M.P. 'charged with deliberation on the common good'.[44]

[41] *Letter to Trower*, 22 March 1818, 7:261.

[42] Ibid.

[43] 'State of the country', p. 299 (italics in original). This kind of argument is, of course, reminiscent of the argument deployed by Whig reformers in parliament in their response to the Six Acts in 1819. In that instance, too, the problem was seen in terms of a failure to apply the *existing* constitutional provisions to the full.

[44] Samuel Beer, 'The representation of interests', pp. 629, 632. According to Beer, the reforms of this whole era ushered in what has been called 'the golden

The inner contradictions, to say nothing of the hypocrisy, of such a theory—a theory which precluded on principle any 'authoritative instructions' or 'mandates' from the electorate outside parliament while practically condoning a private patronage network[45]—called forth some of the most vitriolic denunciations of the unreformed parliament by radicals like James Mill. However, as we have seen, unlike Ricardo neither James Mill nor Mackintosh nor Jeffrey were prepared to challenge substantially the existing theory beyond favouring an expansion of a form of 'virtual' representation of the middle and working classes. In their minds, adjustments in the franchise did not alter the duty of the private M.P. to formulate the common good of the nation in parliament more 'independently', and for him to do this by employing his own deliberate sense of right untainted by the demands (read sinister interests) of his constituents. Thus, in their theories of politics, the duties of a representative superior in judgement to those he represented remained the same. In this way, a reformed parliament remained the sole locus for the conduct of politics understood as the informed deliberation and determination of government policy.

This view of representation and 'politics in parliament' was not substantially altered in the writings of John Stuart Mill. Indeed, it was the hallmark of the younger Mill's attitude towards the duty of the representative that instructive consultations between representatives and constituents were not only unnecessary but also ill-advised.[46] While in his more mature writings on *Representative Government* John Stuart Mill did move to embrace the so-called

---

age of the private M.P.', in which the model M.P. (however far that ideal was removed from actual practice) was the man whose opinion and vote turned on the conscientious adherence to principle rather than patronage. In supporting this notion of representation, Mackintosh objected violently to the alternative model of representation—actual representation. Indeed, he chose to characterize the American practice of that form of representation as founded on 'a ground untenable in argument' whether founded on history, principle, or practice (see his 'Universal suffrage', pp. 200–203 and 'Parliamentary reform', pp. 476–77).

[45] See Beer, 'The representation of interests', pp. 616, 624.

[46] Dennis Thompson has argued that the younger Mill's 1835 'Reflections on the rationale of political representation' explicitly rejected the notion of a delegate theory, arguing that constituents should not ask a representative 'to act according to *their* judgement, any more than they require a physician to prescribe for them according to their own notion of medicine' (quoted in Dennis Thompson's *John Stuart Mill on Representative Government*, p. 112).

Hare plan and to argue for the concept of 'personal representation' (explicitly understood as the representation of ideas), his attitude towards the judgement of constituents regarding policy-making remained unaltered. According to John Stuart Mill, the duty of the representative in parliament was to represent independently and competently those ideas to which he was personally committed. A body of constituents from across the nation, who subscribed to, and sought representation for, those ideas, would vote for him. If elected, however, it was the duty of such constituents to defer to their representative's policy determinations even as they continued to judge the adequacy of his performance. It is fair to say that the younger Mill never embraced the opinion that, once elected, the representative had any need (much less any duty) to consult his constituents periodically in order to gain a clearer understanding of *their* ideas or interests.

Therefore, for both Whig reformers and for radicals like Bentham and the Mills (though they differed dramatically at other points), the motivations and, more important, the knowledge of the electorate and their M.P.s, were taken to be quantitatively and qualitatively different.[47] It remained the duty of an M.P. to shape the national political agenda according to his own best lights, without recurring to his constituents in search of a more directly 'informed' judgement of their material interests.[48] More to the point, even as late as 1861 John Stuart Mill was still prepared to suggest that if the House of Commons were successfully reformed of its corrupting 'courtly or aristocratic atmosphere' then the duration of parliaments ought to be no less than five years, in order to prevent the 'timid subserviency' of representatives to their constituents.[49]

[47] It should be noted that Dennis Thompson has argued that commentators on Mill's later writings actually failed to notice that the principle of competence was balanced by the principle of participation—a principle which, it is implied, would permit constituents to secure pledges from their representative to conform to their sentiments. Yet, as Thompson also observes, Mill's attitude to the delegate theory of representation was consistently negative, and the instances in which Mill recognized the legitimate desires of the electors to extract pledges from the representatives were linked directly to the 'adverse social circumstances or faulty institutions' that existed at the time. In this sense, pledging was clearly not defended by Mill on principle, and Mill never argued that constituents' opinions should shape the representative's behaviour once he was elected (*John Stuart Mill on Representative Government*, pp. 114–15).

[48] John Stuart Mill, *Representative Government*, p. 320.

[49] Ibid., pp. 320–21. Mill continues in this vein: 'As things now are, the period

Ricardo's argument for trienniality is indicative of a rather different view of the duty of representatives and, therefore, of the purposes behind more frequent parliaments. As Ricardo saw it, the best way to reform the older, patronage-based parliament, and 'to destroy the dependence of the former on the executive government', was not to make representatives more 'independent' of influence, but to link them much more closely to their constituents.[50] Indeed, Ricardo seems to have been at his most 'radical', and certainly his most democratic, when arguing that good government could be secured only by ensuring that representatives were 'chosen by the unbiased good sense' of the people, *and* by ensuring that the interests of those representatives should not be permitted to oppose those of their constituents:

> The ability of representatives when their interests are opposed to those of their constituents is a great evil because it can only be employed in promoting objects which are mischievous to the latter.[51]

As far as Ricardo was concerned, therefore, the purpose of bringing representatives more frequently before the people was not at all to render them 'timidly subservient', but to render them directly informed as to their constituents' actual material interests and conditions. More frequent exposure, it must be said, would also go far towards better informing the people of the character and interests of their representatives. This, too, concerned Ricardo. Since, as we have already seen, the direct political implication of Ricardo's economics had been to conceive of the idea of national interest in terms of material prosperity, it was this which led him to propose a reform strategy which was in opposition to the existing presumption that the people inherently lacked the capacity to judge what was conducive to this interest.[52]

In the last analysis, Ricardo's argument for triennial parliaments leads to two main conclusions. The first is that the gulf separating the motivations and capacities for judgement of representatives and their constituents was thought by Ricardo to be considerably less than that posited by other political reformers of the day—

---

of seven years, though of unnecessary length, is hardly worth altering for any benefit likely to be produced' (p. 321).

[50] *Letter to Trower*, 22 March 1818, 7:261.

[51] Ibid., pp. 260–61.

[52] Ricardo, *Parliamentary Reform* 5:499.

Whig or Radical. Just as the political economist could safely rely upon the capacity of ordinary men freely to exercise their economic franchise, the political policymaker could not reasonably doubt the ability of such men freely to exercise the vote. The second is that the difference between Ricardo's perspective on the question of the duration of parliaments and that taken up by others, turned precisely on his own particular vision of political life. The great object of politics, which for Ricardo was advancing material prosperity, was shared *de facto* by everyone engaged in economic life. Indeed, as far as Ricardo was concerned, the basic data of importance to political decision-makers were those material interests and purposive actions of ordinary men. In this sense, economic life was not perceived as the common man's substitute for political life—a life that on the old model was open to but a few. On the contrary, in Ricardo's mind economic life was the very stuff of which politics was constituted. One might go so far as to say that this view of political life makes understandable Ricardo's consistent substitution of the term 'constituent' for that more narrow and antiquated term 'elector' whenever referring to members of the political nation.

However, the substance of Ricardian politics suggested more than just a change in language. The intimate relationship between material and political interests proposed by Ricardo effectively legitimized the claim of the working class that parliamentary politics, as it then existed, failed to consult and register *their* material interests and prosperity in calculating the common good. To consult and register these interests, though not necessarily in every case to satisfy them, was the duty of the representative. When such a union between representative and constituent could be forged, then for Ricardo at least, democracy had been achieved.

It is the hallmark of Ricardian politics that the expressed interests of the various classes of society, no matter how conflictual they might be, should be voiced in parliament. Paradoxically, then, Ricardo might well have thought that James Mackintosh was half right when he declared the idea that 'the value of popular election chiefly depends on the exercise of a deliberate judgement by the electors' to be an 'original fallacy'.[53] For Ricardo, too, the value of popular elections lay not only in the ability of the constituents to

[53] 'Universal suffrage', p. 198.

140

exercise judgement, but in the social and political value of having basic information necessary to political decision-making brought into parliament.

Of course, to be properly understood and accurately evaluated, it needs to be remembered that Ricardo's proposals for the reform of British political life were firmly situated in an early stage in the development of the political reform movement of the nineteenth century—a stage pre-dating the emergence of modern party politics, in the sense of either a disciplined membership or a clearly articulated party platform. When Ricardo wrote to Trower in the spring of 1818 that if elected he would be 'neither Whig nor Tory but should be anxiously desirous of promoting every measure which should give us a chance of good government',[54] he was merely expressing a common attitude towards what were, in this period, little more than loosely structured parliamentary groupings. Burke's definition of a party as 'a body of men united, for promoting by their joint endeavours the national interest, upon some particular principle in which they are all agreed', could as easily have been a self-definition of the whole of parliament itself in the early nineteenth century.[55] It is perhaps for this reason that political conflict within parliament in this period was as often spoken of in terms of the positions taken up on the ministerial and oppositional benches as it was in terms of party alignments. Be that as it may, one thing at least is certain: namely, that any notion of party organization and identification more stringent than that of a loose political grouping of men of common social backgrounds and economic associations would have struck at the very heart of the idea of the 'independent' and 'private' M.P. which guided reformers of all stripes at the time, and which provided the template for Ricardo's own reform proposals. Of course, someway further down the road of political development, the commitment to party government in Britain would effectively preclude the possibility of representatives acting independently—whether in the sense of 'virtual' trustees of the common good or, as Ricardo appears to have hoped, in the sense of direct and institutionally unmediated voices expressing the material interests of *all* of the people.

[54] *Letter to Trower*, 22 March 1818, 7:260.
[55] See Samuel Beer, 'The representation of interests', p. 169.

Conclusion

Thomas babington macaulay's famous indictment of James Mill's thinking about politics may seem to be a somewhat strange item with which to prefigure some final reflections on Ricardian politics. After all, it was in the pages of the March number of the *Edinburgh Review* for 1829, a good six years after Ricardo's death, that Macaulay denounced Mill's attempt to 'deduce' a theory of politics from certain 'propensities of human nature' on the grounds that this endeavour could hardly be said to have ranked him as a contributor to 'that noble Science of Politics'.[1] Yet, while in itself Macaulay's charge is both jejune and brim-full of that familiar Whig air of moral superiority,[2] it does at least convey a fairly accurate sense of the way in which both Bentham and James Mill conceived of the whole programme of the philosophic-radical tendency in the first decades of the nineteenth century.

On the philosophical plane, Bentham and Mill had begun from a model of man quintessentially utilitarian in constitution. Starting with individual agents, it was to their rendition of the science of human nature that they turned in the quest for a science of politics suitable for the modern world. To make the case for the inclusion of larger numbers into the political nation, on this line of reasoning, all that needed to be established was that individuals had the capacity properly to judge their own interests and that they were unencumbered in their ability to act upon them. But if Bentham and Mill were individualists in this philosophical arena, they were neither automatically nor necessarily democrats in the political one. On that subject, everything turned on the question of judging

---

[1] *Mill on Government*, p. 419. There is a close affinity between Macaulay's criticism of Mill and that advanced a little later by Mackintosh (*Ethical Philosophy*, p. 208 et seq.).

[2] A rather different opinion of the value of Macaulay's attack was reached by William Thomas, who has argued that it was 'one of those pieces of controversial writing . . . in which the arguments are so well turned, and the demonstration so conclusive, that they have proved more enduring than the work which provoked them' (*Philosophic Radicals*, p. 136).

when (or if) individual capacity had reached an acceptable standard. This criterion proved to be sufficiently malleable to allow them to appear either as expansive and democratic, or as narrow and elitist, as the case required.[3] In this way, the tensions between utility and democracy were to prove problematic ever after, and never more so perhaps than in the political writings of their distinguished successor John Stuart Mill.

Indeed, when viewed in this light, the subsequent contributions of John Stuart Mill to philosophical radicalism (which, it should not be forgotten, did so much to refine the basis of the utilitarian theory of choice and action that it was a relatively straightforward matter for economists like Jevons and Walras to translate it into mathematics a generation later[4]) seem to fall entirely within the compass of that earlier project. To be sure, the younger Mill also devoted much of his time and effort to an attempt to re-capture for utilitarianism the moral high ground which he felt had been given up rather too readily by his father and by Bentham. Poetry did, after all, have more to recommend it than push-pin, and it was on the whole better to have as a lodger a Socrates unsatisfied, than a pig satisfied. However, in this enterprise the younger Mill seems merely to have been acting out a part in much the same drama in which Adam Smith had played so decisive a role a century earlier. Whatever Bentham and the elder Mill may have conceded to the enemies of utilitarian individualism, Mandeville's scurrilous tales had certainly conceded to the theorists of civic virtue back in the eighteenth century. John Stuart Mill's famous essays on Bentham and Coleridge, and *Utilitarianism*, have in some sense to be understood as an effort to take back some of the same moral territory

[3] A proper recognition of this very basic element of theoretical structure of the utilitarian theory of choice and action, upon which the whole of the science of politics was grounded for Bentham and James Mill, is of more than passing interest. For one thing, it appears to render the great debate which has raged over whether Bentham and Mill were or were not democrats 'in principle' and, if so, which of the two might be said to have been the more democratic (a debate which has generated so much heat), completely irrelevant to the correct assessment of their political theory.

[4] The younger Mill's open recognition of the problems of interpersonal comparisons of utility (in his discussion of the 'harm principle' and elsewhere), and his clear-sighted analytical distinction between issues of efficiency and issues of equity in matters of social choice were, in this context at least, particularly advanced.

for individualism in politics that Smith had sought to recover for self-interested action in the *Theory of Moral Sentiments*. Whether or not this added a new and more satisfactory moral dimension to utilitarian individualism may be the subject of debate; what cannot be doubted is that the fundamental nexus between the science of human nature and the science of politics emerged from the younger Mill's remodelling of utilitarianism intact.

It is precisely when they are set against this framework of concepts, that the ideas and arguments which constitute Ricardo's politics are revealed in their most distinctive form. As we have seen, for Ricardo the task of constructing a new science of politics was inextricably bound up with the science of political economy. For him, the construction of a new science of politics—a science upon which the reform of the existing political constitution was to be built—evidently required a more systematic consideration of the relationship between economic functioning and political organization than attempted by either Bentham or James Mill. There is no doubt that Ricardo was, above all else, an economist. However, there is equally no doubt that he integrated his economics into a systematic view of politics in a way others did not. The impact of his economic analysis on his thinking about politics can be measured in two ways. In his politics, just as in his economics, Ricardo was not strictly a utilitarian, nor was he, in the most important respect, an individualist. It was not utilitarian for the simple reason that in defining the standard of material well-being as aggregate production itself, rather than some aggregate of individual utilities, he shifted the focus of analysis away from individual utility maximizers. It is not individualist, because Ricardo instead focused on the conditions of reproduction and growth, where the relevant actors, for him, were social classes not individual agents, and where the relevant categories were objective economic ones rather than the psychological one of utility. This led him to conceive of the dynamics of politics in terms of an interplay between these larger aggregate interests. As in his economic theory, he saw these interests as being generated by the differing material concerns of these groups, and thus as being both diverse and conflictual. In his political writings, politics became the arena in which these competing claims could be publicly aired, and where conflicting interests could be structured in a stable and representative way.

Of course, there can be no doubt that Ricardian politics took the end of government to be the greatest good, as had Bentham and Mill. Ricardo himself deployed that utilitarian maxim frequently in the course of his writing. But the important point is that while history rightly places all three in the same political camp, that is, in a party whose practical political proposals were (with only minor deviations) the same, from a theoretical perspective Ricardo arrived at these proposals through a conceptual analysis of politics and representation distinctly different from Bentham and Mill.

A direct corollary of this, of course, is that the notion that the foundation of Ricardo's political thought mirrored that of James Mill turns out to be inaccurate in important respects. That he received encouragement from Mill to develop his thinking about politics, is a fact that cannot be doubted. Nor can we doubt the personal importance of this encouragement to Ricardo. However, providing encouragement is not the same thing as providing the substance of an argument. From the evidence presently available it is possible to show that Ricardo developed important aspects of his thinking about politics independently of James Mill. The correct dating of Ricardo's own two discourses on politics, and the recovery of the Ricardo-Trower correspondence against which those two discourses must be understood, provides ample evidence of this fact.[5]

Another implication of the present account of Ricardo's politics,

[5] Although James Bonar and Jacob Hollander published the Ricardo-Trower correspondence in 1899, it was not really until 1952, with the publication of Piero Sraffa's edition of Ricardo's *Works and Correspondence*, that the raw material from which a revision of the opinion could be made was assembled in one place. Apart from the unavailability of all the evidence, another factor contributing to diminish Ricardo's individual contribution, was the tendency of subsequent interpreters and historians to emphasise James Mill's intellectual leadership of the philosophic-radical tendency which both Mill himself, and his son, indulged in from time to time. It often appears that subsequent generations of scholars have taken these sources as the final arbiters on the matter—and this to the detriment of the historical record. The exception is William Thomas who in his *Philosophic Radicals* in 1979 broke with the tradition and at least admitted the possibility that Ricardo might have made an independent contribution (p. 126). Thomas, however, stays within the received wisdom when he claims that 'the basic argument for an extended franchise, the need to find an electorate smaller than the whole community but still with the interests of the whole community at heart, is the same in both' (p. 126). Our own argument, of course, would suggest that this is an opinion that needs now to be adjusted.

is that it serves also to highlight the limitations of those readings of Ricardo which represent him as fashioning little more than a sustained defence of the interests of the capitalist class against the claims (whether in the economic or the political sphere) of either the land-owning classes or the working class.[6]

While on this subject, it will not have escaped the notice of the attentive reader of the foregoing pages that there is one key feature of Ricardo's economics which has not figured at all in our account of his thinking about politics; namely, the labour theory of value. This seemingly curious fact, it might be thought, stands in need of some explanation. After all, it is well-enough known that the Ricardian Socialists of subsequent generations used the labour theory of value in order to launch their claim to labour's 'right to the whole produce of labour', to borrow the title of Anton Menger's celebrated book. (Although there is some debate as to whether their real source and inspiration might not have been Adam Smith rather than Ricardo.) Moreover, successive generations of Marxists have chosen to regard the labour theory of value as the lynch-pin of their whole critique of the capitalist system. And this not without cause, since the labour theory of value was re-modelled by Marx so that it could function as the lens through which was revealed the 'true' character of the social relations that permeated what he called 'the hidden abode of production'. Even the critics of Marx (beginning with Böhm-Bawerk) seem to have been agreed about the importance of the labour theory of value to the political message of Marx; but they, of course, concentrated on highlighting its not inconsiderable analytical weaknesses in their endeavour to short-circuit the revolutionary conclusions that were being drawn from it. Indeed, when the *Works and Correspondence of David Ricardo* were finally published, one reviewer went so far as to wonder whether the Moscow State Publishing House might not have been an equally appropriate sponsor of that enterprise as the Royal Economic Society (under whose auspices the edition was in fact prepared).[7] Now, quite apart from whether the labour theory of value is actually capable of carrying the weight

[6] Of course, this does not mean that one would wish to go quite as far as Lionel Robbins seems to have done in suggesting that Ricardo uniformly had only the interest of workers uppermost in his mind (*The Theory of Economic Policy*, p. 83).

[7] T. W. Hutchison: 'Some questions about Ricardo', p. 421.

the various partisan causes in whose support it has been mustered would have us place upon it, the historical record alone is sufficient to prompt a polite inquiry as to why it is that the present account of Ricardo's politics has accorded so little place to such an apparently powerful economic argument.

At one level an explanation is easy enough to provide: no appeal to the labour theory of value is to be found in any part of Ricardo's own contributions to political thought. Should one wish to ask why this might be so,[8] the answer would require arguments of a more speculative character than any we have made before, since Ricardo said nothing whatsoever about the matter himself. There is, however, one particular avenue through which this question might be addressed that does seem to offer some promise of success; it is opened up by reflecting for a moment on the analytical role of the labour theory of value in Ricardian economics itself.

For Ricardo the 'principal problem in Political Economy' was to 'determine the laws which regulate . . . distribution',[9] and those laws (as we have seen) were germane to the shaping of his thinking about politics in a multitude of ways. The theory of value, and the labour theory of value in particular, was the necessary analytical apparatus for discovering these laws. But in an important sense questions concerning the distribution of social production were considered by Ricardo himself to be separable from those concerning value. In the limited confines of the *Essay on Profits* in 1815, for example, Ricardo had in fact constructed his entire theory of distribution without recourse to the theory of value at all. This, thanks to his assumption that in agriculture the same commodity, corn, appeared as both the means of production (corn wages) and as output, so that the rate of profit of the farmer (determined on land that commanded no rent) regulated the profits of all other trades.[10] Thus was the principal problem of political economy settled within the confines of the *Essay on Profits*; and there was no need for a theory of value. Rent was the consequence of the differential fertilities of land successively brought under cultivation,

---

[8] According to Gunnar Myrdal this was the really interesting question; '[T]he classical theory of value leads inevitably to rationalist radicalism, if not necessarily in Marx's formulation, at any rate in that direction' (*The Political Element in the Development of Economic Theory*, p. 79).

[9] *Principles*, 1:5.

[10] *Essay on Profits*, 4:23–24. See also *Letter to Trower*, 8 March 1814, 6:104.

corn wages were determined by customary subsistence requirements, and the rate of profit by 'the proportion of production to
the consumption necessary to such production'.[11] The vision of
conflictual economic relations this approach to distribution entailed was that which Ricardo maintained throughout his life, and
it was that vision by which his politics were informed. As he wrote
to McCulloch (in a famous letter) in 1820:

> After all, the great questions of Rent, Wages, and Profits must be
> explained by the proportions in which the whole produce is divided
> between landlords, capitalists, and labourers, and which are not es-
> sentially connected with the doctrine of value.[12]

Of course, however, these 'proportions' were precisely where
the analytical difficulty lay. If, for example, the rate of profit was
to be determined by the 'proportion' of production to necessary
consumption, then the moment one stepped outside the one-com-
modity world of the *Essay on Profits*, and recognised that both
production and necessary consumption consisted of a collection of
heterogeneous commodities, then the whole thing had to be put
rather differently. The rate of profit now became the 'proportion'
of the *value* of production to the *value* of necessary consumption.
And this is where the labour theory of value enters into the picture
in the *Principles*. But, and this is what is relevant to us at present,
once it has done its analytical job, the theory of distribution takes
on essentially the same character as it had before. This, one might
conjecture, explains Ricardo's focus on distribution rather than on
value in his discussion of politics.

None of this is to say that the labour theory of value would necessarily stand at odds with some of the most prominent themes in
Ricardian politics. By according ordinary labourers a certain priority in the creation of material wealth, it melds fairly well with
the Ricardian impulse towards giving expression to their voices in
a democratic polity. By placing a positive value on their contribution to the production of commodities, it is congruent with the
Ricardian notion that participation in economic life has a value and
provides information which ought in justice to be reflected in political life as well. By implicitly embedding a conflict of class inter-

[11] *Letter to Malthus*, 26 June 1814, 6:108.
[12] *Letter to McCulloch*, 13 June 1820, 8:194.

est in the process of production itself, it matches quite well the familiar Ricardian image of the class structure of capitalist society and the inherently conflictual nature of politics. But it was others, not Ricardo, who were to take up and develop explicitly the political implications of the labour theory of value.

Despite an essentially conflictual view of distribution, Ricardo single-mindedly advocated full democratic participation within the *existing* capitalist scheme. It was not necessary first to consult the degree to which individual intellectual and moral education had spread among the mass of the population before conferring upon them the franchise, it could safely be achieved there and then; in England, in 1819. Against existing theories of virtual representation he brought forward a modern version of the doctrine of class equality. Although he confined his definition of good government to an economistic conception of material prosperity, he did so because he believed that such prosperity was in the interest of all classes. He never once seems to have entertained a doubt that capitalism could survive democracy (something which cannot, it seems, be said with equal certainty of his philosophic-radical friends).

In the last analysis, one is left with the feeling that there is something of a paradox at the very heart of Ricardian politics; one which mirrors almost exactly the paradox that lies at the core of his economic theory, and which many a commentator on Ricardo before us has found cause to notice.

> Ricardo, an orthodox economist, laid down the principles which were adopted by Socialists to upset his own assumptions.[13]

Within living memory of Ricardo's death, his economics was being used to propagate 'dangerous doctrines' and to articulate the political aspirations of the working classes. In the hands of Marx, Ricardo's economics formed the basis of an argument not for reform, but for the revolutionary transformation of society; for the very abolition of the system of private property to which Ricardo had declared himself so wholeheartedly committed. In Ricardo's politics, such a transformation was neither necessary nor inevitable; and this largely because he seems to have relied on a very confident projection of the ability of the economic system to hold con-

---

[13] Leslie Stephen, *The English Utilitarians* 2:188.

flict over the distribution of material production within stable boundaries. His confidence sprung from his immersion in the economic and political life of the times, rather than from any hypothetical model of man and society. It would be left for history to judge whether Ricardian politics was well founded. As Ricardo wrote:

> The grand cause, good government, is always present to my mind, but I hope it will have a better champion in the House of Commons. In every argument with my friends I do what I can to maintain the cause of truth, as far as I can see it, and frequently flatter myself that I am successful. I am quite sure that the good cause is advancing, though at a very moderate step, and all we can hope to do in our time is to help it a little forward.[14]

A week after writing these lines, Ricardo was confined to his bed at Gatcomb Park with 'an illness originating from a cold in the ear'.[15] He died five days later, on 11 September 1823, never having witnessed the passage of a single measure of parliamentary reform during his lifetime.[16]

[14] *Letter to Mill*, 30 August 1823, 9:325.

[15] *Works and Correspondence* 9:388.

[16] This pleasure was not denied to Bentham who, though his death came the day before the passage of the 1832 Reform Bill, lived to see the repeal of the Corporation and Test Acts as well as Catholic Emancipation. Nor was it denied to James Mill, who died in 1836.

✤ Bibliography ✤

Adams, George Burton, and H. Morse Stephens, eds. 1947. *Select Documents in English Constitutional History*. London: Macmillan.

Aspinall, Arthur. 1927. *Lord Brougham and the Whig Party*. Manchester: Manchester University Press.

Bagehot, Walter. 1879. *Economic Studies*. Reprinted, Academic Reprints: Stanford, 1953.

Bamford, Samuel. 1905. *'Passages in the Life of a Radical' and 'Early Days'*. Edited and abridged in two volumes by Henry Dunckley. London: T. Fisher Unwin. First published in 1841 and 1848, respectively.

Beer, Max. 1929. *A History of British Socialism*. 2 vols. Revised edition. London: G. Bell and Sons Ltd. (1st English ed., 1919; 1st German ed., 1912).

Beer, Samuel H. 1957. 'The representation of interests in British government: historical background'. *American Political Science Review* 51(3) (September): 613–50.

Beer, Samuel. H. 1969. *British Politics in the Collectivist Age*. New York: Vintage (1st published, 1965).

Bentham, Jeremy. 1776. *A Fragment on Government or A Comment on the Commentaries & Etc.* In the Bowring edition of *Works*, 1:221–95.

———. 1817. *A Plan for Parliamentary Reform in the Form of a Catechism & Etc.* In Bowring's edition of *Works* 3:533–57.

———. 1832. *Lord Brougham Displayed & Etc.* In the Bowring edition of *Works* 5:548–612.

———. 1838–1843. *The Works of Jeremy Bentham*. Edited in 10 vols. by John Bowring. Reprinted, New York: Russell and Russell, 1962.

———. 1952. *Jeremy Bentham's Economic Writings*. 3 vols. Edited by W. Stark. London: George Allen & Unwin.

Black, Eugene C., ed. 1969. *British Politics in the Nineteenth Century*. New York: Harper and Row.

Black, R.D.C. 1960. *Economic Thought and the Irish Question: 1817–1870*. Cambridge: Cambridge University Press.

Blake, William. 1823. *Observations on the Effects Produced by the Expenditure of Government During the Restriction of Cash Payments*. London: John Murray.

Blaug, Mark. 1958. *Ricardian Economics: A Historical Study*. New Haven: Yale University Press.

Bonar, James, and Jacob H. Hollander, eds. 1899. *Letters of David Ricardo to Hutches Trower and Others: 1811–1823*. Oxford: Clarendon Press.

Brady, Alexander. 1928. *William Huskisson and Liberal Reform.* London: Humphrey Milford (publisher to Oxford University Press).

Briggs, Asa. 1956. 'Middle-class consciousness in English politics'. *Past and Present* 9 (April): 65–74.

———. 1959. *The Age of Improvement: 1783–1867.* Published in the United States under the title *The Making of Modern England: 1783–1867*, New York: Harper & Row.

Brinton, Crane. 1949. *English Political Thought in the Nineteenth Century.* Cambridge, Mass.: Harvard University Press.

[Brougham, Henry]. 1855–1860. *The Works of Henry Lord Brougham and Vaux.* 11 vols. London and Glasgow: Richard Griffin and Company. (Re-issued with a biographical memoir, Edinburgh: Adam and Charles Black, 1872.)

———. 1855. *Dissertations and Addresses: Rhetorical and Literary.* In Brougham's *Works*, vol. 7.

———. 1856. *Historical Sketches of Statesmen who Flourished in the Time of George III.* 3 vols., in Brougham's *Works*, vols. 3, 4, & 5. (Originally published, London: 1839.)

Burke, Edmund. 1791. *An Appeal from the New to the Old Whigs & Etc.* In *Works* 3:331–457.

———. 1796. *Three Letters . . . On the Proposals for Peace with the Regicide Directory of France.* In *Works* 4:331–554.

———. 1839. *The Works of Edmund Burke.* 9 vols. Boston: Charles C. Little and James Brown.

Burrow, J. W. 1988. *Whigs and Liberals: Continuity and Change in English Political Thought.* Oxford: Clarendon Press.

Buxton, Sidney. 1888. *Finance and Politics: An Historical Study, 1783–1885.* London: John Murray. Reprinted, New York: Augustus M. Kelley, 1966.

Cannan, Edwin. 1894. 'Ricardo in Parliament: I & II'. *Economic Journal* 4(14) & 4(15) (June & September): 249–61, 409–23.

———. 1917. *A History of the Theories of Production and Distribution in English Political Economy from 1776 to 1848.* 3d ed. London: P. S. King & Son Ltd. (1st ed., 1893).

[Canning, George]. 1829. *Memoirs of the Life of the Right Honourable George Canning.* 2d ed. 2 vols.. London: Thomas Tegg.

Carlyle, Thomas. 1829. 'Signs of the times'. Reprinted in *Critical and Miscellaneous Essays.* 7 vols. London: Chapman and Hall, 1869 (1st published, 1839). Vol. 2, pp. 230–52.

Carr, Wendell Robert. 1971. 'James Mill's politics reconsidered: parliamentary reform and the triumph of truth'. *The Historical Journal* 14(3):553–80.

Claeys, Gregory. 1987. *Machinery, Money and the Millennium: From*

Moral Economy to Socialism, 1815–1860. Princeton: Princeton University Press.

――――. 1989. *Citizens and Saints: Politics and Anti-politics in Early British Socialism*. Cambridge: Cambridge University Press.

Coats, A. W. 1967. 'The classical economists and the labourer', as reprinted in A. W. Coats (ed).: *The Classical Economists and Economic Policy* (1971), pp. 144–79.

――――, ed. 1971. *The Classical Economists and Economic Policy*. London: Methuen & Co. Ltd.

Cockburn, Henry. 1852. *The Life of Lord Jeffrey, With a Selection from His Correspondence*. 2 vols. Edinburgh: Adam and Charles Black.

Cole, G.D.H. 1938. *Persons and Periods: Studies*. London: Macmillan.

Collini, Stefan, Donald Winch, and John Burrow. 1983. *That Noble Science of Politics*. Cambridge: Cambridge University Press.

Cook, Christopher, and John Stevenson. 1980. *British Historical Facts: 1760–1830*. London: Macmillan.

Corry, Bernard A. 1962. *Money, Saving and Investment in English Economics: 1800–1850*. London: Macmillan.

Cunningham, William. 1903. *The Growth of English Industry and Commerce*. 3 vols. Cambridge: Cambridge University Press.

Davidson, William L. 1916. *Political Thought in England: The Utilitarians From Bentham to J. S. Mill*. New York: Henry Holt & Co. London: Williams and Norgate.

De Quincey, Thomas. 1821. *Confessions of an English Opium-Eater*. In *Works*, vol. 1.

――――. 1878. *The Works of Thomas De Quincey*. 4th ed. 16 vols. Edinburgh: Adam and Charles Black.

De Vivo, Giancarlo. 1984. *Ricardo and His Critics*. Modena: Studi e ricerche dell'Instituto Economico; No. 23.

Dickinson, H. T. 1977. *Liberty and Property: Political Ideology in Eighteenth-century Britain*. New York: Holmes and Meier; London: Weidenfeld and Nicolson.

Dixon, Peter. 1976. *George Canning: Politician and Statesman*. New York: Mason/Charter.

Dobb, Maurice H. 1973. *Theories of Value and Distribution Since Adam Smith*. Cambridge: Cambridge University Press.

Fay, Charles Ryle. 1951. *Huskisson and His Age*. London: Longmans Green and Co.

Fetter, Frank Whitson. 1965. *Development of British Monetary Orthodoxy: 1797–1875*. Reprinted, Fairfield (N.J.): Augustus M. Kelley, 1978.

――――. 1975. 'The influence of economists in parliament on British legislation from Ricardo to John Stuart Mill'. *Journal of Political Economy* 83(5) (October): 1051–64.

———. 1980. *The Economist in Parliament: 1780–1868*. Durham (N.C.): Duke University Press.

Finer, S. E. 1952. *The Life and Times of Sir Edwin Chadwick*. London: Methuen & Company.

Flora, Peter et al., eds. 1983. *State, Economy, and Society in Western Europe: 1815–1975*. 2 vols. London: Macmillan.

Fontana, Biancamaria. 1985. *Rethinking the Politics of Commercial Society: The Edinburgh Review 1802–1832*. Cambridge: Cambridge University Press.

Friedman, Milton. 1982. *Capitalism and Freedom*. Re-issued with new Preface. Chicago: University of Chicago Press (1st ed., 1962).

Gash, Norman. 1961. *Mr. Secretary Peel: The Life of Sir Robert Peel to 1830*. London: Longman.

Gordon, Barry. 1976. *Political Economy in Parliament 1819–1823*. London: Macmillan.

———. 1979. *Economic Doctrine and Tory Liberalism 1824–1830*. London: Macmillan.

Gore, John, ed. 1934. *Creevy's Life and Times: A Further Selection from the Correspondence of Thomas Creevey*. London: John Murray.

Grampp, William D. 1948. 'On the politics of the classical economists'. *Quarterly Journal of Economics* 62(5):714–47.

Green, R. H. 1982. 'Money, output and inflation in classical economics'. *Contributions to Political Economy* 1 (March): 59–85.

Halévy, Elie. 1903. *Thomas Hodgskin*. English edition, edited with an introduction by A. J. Taylor, London: Ernest Benn Ltd., 1956.

———. 1913–1932. *A History of the English People in the Nineteenth Century*. 2d English ed. Translated in 6 vols. by E. I. Watkin and D. A. Barker. London: Ernest Benn, 1960–1961.

———. 1928. *The Growth of Philosophic Radicalism*. 1st (French) ed., 1900–1904. English edition, reprinted New York: Augustus M. Kelley, 1972.

Hamburger, Joseph. 1962. 'James Mill on universal suffrage and the middle class'. *Journal of Politics* 24(1) (February): 167–90.

———. 1963. *James Mill and the Art of Revolution*. New Haven: Yale University Press.

———. 1965. *Intellectuals in Politics: John Stuart Mill and the Philosophic Radicals*. New Haven: Yale University Press.

Hargreaves, E. L. 1930. *The National Debt*. London: Edward Arnold & Co.

Harrison, Ross. 1983. *Bentham*. London: Routledge & Kegan Paul.

Hawes, Frances. 1957. *Henry Brougham*. London: Jonathan Cape.

Hilton, Boyd. 1977. *Corn, Cash, Commerce: The Economic Policies of the Tory Governments 1815–1830*. Oxford: Oxford University Press.

Himes, James. 1928. 'The place of John Stuart Mill and of Robert Owen in the history of English Neo-Malthusianism'. *Quarterly Journal of Economics* 42 (August): 627–40.

Hollander, Samuel. 1979. *The Economics of David Ricardo*. London: Heinemann.

———. 1987. *Classical Economics*. Oxford: Basil Blackwell.

Hone, J. Ann. 1982. *For the Cause of Truth: Radicalism in London, 1796–1821*. Oxford: Clarendon Press.

Hovell, Mark. 1925. *The Chartist Movement*. 2d ed. Manchester: Manchester University Press (1st ed. 1917).

Hutchison, T. W. 1952. 'Some questions about Ricardo'. *Economica*, New Series, 19(76) (November): 415–32.

Jeffrey, Francis. 1819. 'State of the country'. *Edinburgh Review* 32(64):293–309.

Judd, Gerrit P. IV. 1955. *Members of Parliament: 1734–1832*. New Haven: Yale University Press.

Keynes, John Maynard. 1936. *The General Theory of Employment, Interest and Money*. London: Macmillan.

———. 1951. *Essays in Biography*. 2d ed. Edited by Geoffrey Keynes. New York: W. W. Norton (1st ed. 1933).

Macaulay, Thomas Babington. 1829. 'Mill on government'. *Edinburgh Review*, March; as reprinted in *Miscellaneous Writings* 1: 388–419.

Maccoby, S. 1955. *English Radicalism 1786–1832: From Paine to Cobbett*. London: George Allen & Unwin.

McCulloch, J. R. 1827. 'Rise, progress, present state, and prospects of the British cotton manufacture'. *Edinburgh Review* 46 (June): 1–39.

Maccunn, John. 1910. *Six Radical Thinkers & Etc*. London: Edward Arnold.

Mackintosh, James. 1818. 'Universal suffrage'. *Edinburgh Review* 31(61) (December): 165–203.

———. 1820. 'Parliamentary Reform'. *Edinburgh Review* 34(68) (November): 461–502.

———. 1832. *A General View of the Progress of Ethical Philosophy & Etc*. Philadelphia: Carey and Lee.

Malthus, Thomas Robert. 1836. *Principles of Political Economy, Considered With a View to their Practical Application*. 2d ed. (published posthumously), reprinted with an introduction by Morton Paglin. New York: Augustus M. Kelley, 1951. (1st ed. 1820).

Marcet, Jane. 1821. *Conversations on Political Economy, in Which the Elements of that Science are Familiarly Explained*. 4th ed. London: Longman, Hurst, Rees, Orme, and Brown. (1st ed. 1816).

155

Marshall, Alfred. 1920. *Principles of Economics*. 8th ed. London: Macmillan (1st ed. 1890).

Marshall, T. H. 1949. 'Citizenship and social class'. Reprinted in his *Class, Citizenship and Social Development*. Chicago: University of Chicago Press (1977), pp. 71–134.

Martineau, Harriet. 1877. *A History of the Thirty Years' Peace: AD 1816–1846*. 4 vols. Reprint (with corrections) of the 1858 ed. London: George Bell and Sons.

Marx, Karl. 1843. *Critique of Hegel's Doctrine of the State*. In Lucio Colletti, ed. *Karl Marx: Early Writings*. New York: Vintage, 1975.

———. 1852. *The Eighteenth Brumaire of Louis Bonaparte*. New York: International Publishers, 1963.

———. 1862–1863. *Theories of Surplus Value*. 3 vols. Moscow: Progress Publishers, 1963.

———. 1974. *Surveys from Exile*. Edited by David Fernbach. New York: Vintage.

Marx, Karl, and Fredrick Engels. 1942. *Selected Correspondence: 1846–1895*. Reprinted, Westport: Greenwood Press, 1975.

Maxwell, Herbert, ed. 1904. *The Creevy Papers: A Selection from the Correspondence and Diaries of the Late Thomas Creevy, M.P.* 2 vols. London: John Murray.

Meek, Ronald L. 1950. 'The decline of Ricardian economics in England'. *Economica*, New Series, February, pp. 43–62.

Milgate, Murray. 1982. *Capital and Employment*. London & New York: Academic Press.

Mill, James. 1804. *An Essay on the Impolicy of a Bounty on the Exportation of Grain & Etc*. London: C & R Baldwin. Reprinted New York: Augustus M. Kelley, 1966.

———. 1808. *Commerce Defended*. Reprinted, New York: Augustus M. Kelley, 1965.

———. 1812. *Schools for All, in Preference to Schools for Churchmen Only*. First published in *The Philanthropist*, and reprinted in W. H. Burston, ed.: *James Mill on Education*. Cambridge: Cambridge University Press, 1969.

———. 1817. *Colony*. In the Supplement to the 4th, 5th, & 6th editions of the *Encyclopedia Britannica* (1816–1824), 3:257–73.

———. 1818a. *Economists*. In the Supplement to the 4th, 5th, & 6th editions of the *Encyclopedia Britannica* (1816–1824), 3:703–24.

———. 1818b. *Education*. First published in the Supplement to the 4th, 5th, & 6th editions of the *Encyclopedia Britannica* (1816–1824) and reprinted in W. H. Burston, ed.: *James Mill on Education*. Cambridge: Cambridge University Press, 1969.

———. 1820. *Government*. First published in the Supplement to the

4th, 5th, & 6th editions of the *Encyclopedia Britannica* (1816–1824) and reprinted in James Mill: *Essays & Etc.* (1825).

————. 1821. *Liberty of the Press*. First published in the Supplement to the 4th, 5th, & 6th editions of the *Encyclopedia Britannica* (1816–1824) and reprinted in James Mill: *Essays & Etc*. (1825).

————. 1825. *Essays on Government, Jurisprudence, Liberty of the Press and Law of Nations*. London: J. Innes. Reprinted, New York: Augustus M. Kelley, 1967.

————. 1826a. *Elements of Political Economy*. 3rd ed. London: Baldwin, Cradock & Joy (1st ed.: 1818).

————. 1826b. 'Summary review of the conduct and measures of the Seventh Imperial Parliament'. *Parliamentary History and Review*.

————. 1827. 'Constitutional legislation'. *Parliamentary Review*, Sessions of 1826–1827 and 1827–1828. London: Baldwin & Cradock. Pp. 335–74.

————. 1830. 'The ballot'. *Westminster Review* 13(27) (July): 1–39.

————. 1835. *A Fragment on Mackintosh: Being Strictures on Some Passages in the Dissertation by Sir James Mackintosh, Prefixed to the Encyclopedia Britannica*. London: Baldwin and Cradock.

Mill, John Stuart. 1824. 'War expenditure'. *Westminster Review* 2 (July): 27–48.

————. 1835. 'M. de Tocqueville on Democracy in America: Volume I'. *London Review* 2 (October): 85–129. Reprinted in Gertrude Himmelfarb, ed.: *Essays on Politics and Culture: John Stuart Mill*. Gloucester (Mass.): Peter Smith, 1973.

————. 1838. 'Bentham'. *London and Westminster Review* 31 (August). Reprinted in Gertrude Himmelfarb, ed.: *Essays on Politics and Culture: John Stuart Mill*. Gloucester (Mass.): Peter Smith, 1973.

————. 1839. 'Reorganization of the reform party'. *London and Westminster Review* 32 (April): 475–508. Reprinted in Gertrude Himmelfarb, ed.: *Essays on Politics and Culture: John Stuart Mill*. Gloucester (Mass.): Peter Smith, 1973.

————. 1840. 'M. de Tocqueville on Democracy in America: Volume II'. *Edinburgh Review* 72 (October): 1–47. Reprinted in Gertrude Himmelfarb, ed.: *Essays on Politics and Culture: John Stuart Mill*. Gloucester (Mass.): Peter Smith, 1973.

————. 1845. 'Review of Arthur Helps: *The Claims of Labour: An Essay on the Duty of the Employers to the Employed*'. *Edinburgh Review* 81 (April): 498–525. (Also partly reprinted in Mill's *Dissertations and Discussions* (1859). 2 vols. Volume 2, pp. 181–217.)

————. 1861. *Considerations on Representative Government*. Reprinted in *John Stuart Mill: Three Essays & Etc*. Oxford: Oxford University Press, 1975.

Mill, John Stuart. 1863. *Utilitarianism*. 2d ed. 1871. First published in three parts in *Fraser's Magazine* (1861). Reprinted, London: George Routledge & Sons, 1895.

———. 1871. *Principles of Political Economy*. 7th ed. (1st ed. 1848). London: Longmans, 1909.

———. 1873. *Autobiography*. Reprinted, New York: Columbia University Press, 1924.

———. 1874. *Essays on Some Unsettled Questions in Political Economy*. London: Longmans, Green, Reader, and Dyer.

Mitchell, B. R. 1988. *British Historical Statistics*. Cambridge: Cambridge University Press.

Mitchell, B. R., and Phyllis Deane. 1962. *Abstract of British Historical Statistics*. Cambridge: Cambridge University Press.

Myrdal, Gunnar. 1954. *The Political Element in the Development of Economic Theory*. Reprinted, New York: Clarion, 1969 (1st ed. in Swedish, 1929).

Nesbitt, George L. 1934. *Benthamite Reviewing: The First Twelve Years of the Westminster Review, 1824–1836*. New York: Columbia University Press.

The New Palgrave: A Dictionary of Economics. Edited by John Eatwell, Murray Milgate and Peter Newman. 4 vols. London: Macmillan, 1987.

O'Brien, D. P. 1975. *The Classical Economists*. Oxford: Clarendon Press.

Oldfield, T.H.B. 1816. *The Representative History of Great Britain and Ireland: Being a History of the House of Commons & Etc*. 6 vols. London: Baldwin, Cradock, and Joy.

Owen, Robert. 1816. *A New View of Society or Essays on the Formation of the Human Character & Etc*. Reprinted, with an introduction by John Saville. London: Macmillan, 1972.

The Parliamentary Debates From the Year 1803 to the Present Time: Forming a Continuation & Etc. Published under the superintendence of T. C. Hansard: London (various volumes).

Patterson, M. W. 1931. *Sir Francis Burdett and His Times (1770–1844)*. London: Macmillan.

Plamenatz, John. 1958. *The English Utilitarians*. 2d ed. Oxford: Basil Blackwell (1st ed. 1949).

Pope, Rex, ed. 1989. *Atlas of British Social and Economic History Since c. 1700*. London: Routledge.

Pringle-Pattison, A. Seth. 1907. *The Philosophical Radicals and Other Essays & Etc*. Edinburgh and London: William Blackwood and Sons.

Ravenstone, Piercy. 1824. *Thoughts on the Funding System and Its Effects*. London: J. Andrews. Reprinted, New York: Augustus M. Kelley, 1966.

Read, Samuel. 1829. *Political Economy: An Inquiry into the Natural*

Grounds of Right to Vendible Property, or Wealth. Reprinted, Fairfield (N.J.): Augustus M. Kelley, 1976.

Ricardo, David. 1810. *The High Price of Bullion, A Proof of the Depreciation of Banknotes.* (2d ed. 1811). In *Works and Correspondence* 3:47–127.

———. 1811. *Reply to Mr. Bosanquet's Practical Observations on the Report of the Bullion Committee.* In *Works and Correspondence* 3:155–256.

———. 1815. *An Essay on the Influence of a Low Price of Corn on the Profits of Stock.* In *Works and Correspondence* 4:1–42.

———. 1816. *Proposals for an Economical and Secure Currency.* In *Works and Correspondence* 4:43–141.

———. [1820]. *Notes on Mr Malthus work "Principles of Political Economy, considered with a view to their practical application".* In *Works and Correspondence,* vol. 2.

———. 1821. *The Principles of Political Economy and Taxation.* 3d ed. In *Works and Correspondence,* vol. 1. (1st ed., 1817).

———. 1822. *On Protection to Agriculture.* In *Works and Correspondence:* 4:207–70.

———. 1823. *On Blake's 'Observations on the Effects Produced by the Expenditure of Government'.* In *Works and Correspondence* 4:323–56.

———. 1824a. *Defence of the Plan of Voting by Ballot.* In *Works and Correspondence* 5:504–12.

———. 1824b. *Observations on Parliamentary Reform.* In *Works and Correspondence* 5:495–503.

———. 1824c. *Plan for the Establishment of a National Bank.* In *Works and Correspondence* 4:275–97.

———. 1951–1973. *The Works and Correspondence of David Ricardo.* 11 vols. Edited by Piero Sraffa with the collaboration of Maurice H. Dobb. Cambridge: Cambridge University Press.

Robbins, Lionel C. 1961. *The Theory of Economic Policy in English Classical Political Economy.* London: Macmillan.

[Romilly, Samuel]. 1840. *Memoirs of the Life of Sir Samuel Romilly.* 2d ed. Edited in three volumes by his sons. London: John Murray.

Rosenblum, Nancy L. 1978. *Bentham's Theory of the Modern State.* Cambridge, Mass.: Harvard University Press.

Roseveare, Henry. 1973. *The Treasury 1660–1870: The Foundations of Control.* London: George Allen & Unwin.

Samuelson, Paul. 1978. 'The canonical classical model of political economy'. *Journal of Economic Literature* 18: 1415–34.

Schumpeter, Joseph. 1954. *History of Economic Analysis.* New York: Oxford University Press.

Shelley, Percy Bysshe. 1819. 'The masque of anarchy'. In the Ingpen and Peck edition of *Complete Works* 3:225–50.

———. 1819–1820. *A Philosophical View of Reform*. In the Ingpen and Peck edition of the *Complete Works* 7:1–55.

———. 1965. *The Complete Works of Percy Bysshe Shelley*. Edited in ten volumes by Roger Ingpen and Walter E. Peck. London: Ernest Benn. New York: Gordian Press.

Shoup, Carl S. 1960. *Ricardo on Taxation*. New York: Columbia University Press.

Smith, Adam. 1776. *An Inquiry Into the Nature and Causes of the Wealth of Nations*. Edited in two volumes by R. H. Campbell and A. S. Skinner. Oxford: Oxford University Press, 1976.

Stephen, Leslie. 1900. *The English Utilitarians*. 3 vols. Reprinted, New York: Peter Smith, 1950.

Stigler, George J. 1953. 'Sraffa's Ricardo'. *American Economic Review* 43 (September). As reprinted in G. J. Stigler: *Essays in the History of Economics*. Chicago: University of Chicago Press, 1965. Pp. 302–25.

Stimson, Shannon C. 1989. 'Republicanism and the recovery of the political in Adam Smith'. In M. Milgate and C. B. Welch, eds.: *Critical Issues in Social Thought*. London & New York: Academic Press, pp. 91–112.

Stokes, Eric. 1959. *The English Utilitarians and India*. Oxford: Oxford University Press.

Strachey, Lytton. 1922. *Books and Characters: French and English*. London: Chatto & Windus.

Thomas, William. 1969. 'James Mill's politics: the 'Essay on Government' and the movement for reform'. *Historical Journal* 12(2):249–84.

———. 1979. *The Philosophic Radicals: Nine Studies in Theory and Practice: 1817–1841*. Oxford: Clarendon Press.

Thompson, Dennis F. 1976. *John Stuart Mill and Representative Government*. Princeton: Princeton University Press.

Thompson, E. P. 1968. *The Making of the English Working Class*. Revised ed. Harmondsworth: Penguin (1st ed. 1963).

Thompson, Thomas Perronet. 1830. 'Radical reform'. *Westminster Review* 12 (January): 222–32.

Tocqueville, Alexis de. 1835 & 1840. *Democracy in America*. Edited by J. P. Mayer. Two volumes in one. New York: Anchor, 1969.

Tooke, Thomas. 1848. *A History of Prices and of the State of Circulation From 1839 to 1847 & Etc*. London: Longman, Brown, Green, and Longmans.

Toynbee, Arnold. 1884. *Lectures on the Industrial Revolution in England*. With a memoir by B. Jowett. London: Rivingtons.

Tucker, G.S.L. 1960. *Progress and Profits in British Economic Thought.* Cambridge: Cambridge University Press.

Wallas, Graham. 1925. *The Life of Francis Place.* 4th ed. London: George Allen & Unwin (1st ed. 1898).

Walpole, Spencer. 1889. *The Life of Lord John Russell.* 2 vols. London: Longmans, Green & Co. Reprinted, New York: Greenwood Press, 1968.

Weatherall, David. 1976. *David Ricardo: A Biography.* Amsterdam: Martinus Nijhoff.

The Wellesley Index to Victorian Periodicals. Edited by Walter E. Houghton (with the fifth volume by J. H. Slingerland). 5 vols. Toronto: University of Toronto Press (1966–1989).

White, R. J. 1957. *Waterloo to Peterloo.* London: William Heinemann.

Winch, Donald. 1965. *Classical Political Economy and the Colonies.* Cambridge, Mass.: Harvard University Press.

———. 1987. *Malthus.* Oxford: Oxford University Press.

Wrigley, E. A. 1987. *People, Cities and Wealth: The Transformation of Traditional Society.* Oxford: Basil Blackwell.

✛ Index ✛